t 35,

p 15

D1295815

In Defence of Liberalism

For Anne

In Defence of Liberalism

D. A. LLOYD THOMAS

Basil Blackwell

Copyright © D. A. Lloyd Thomas 1988
First published 1988
Basil Blackwell Ltd
108 Cowley Road, Oxford, OX4 1JF, UK

Basil Blackwell Inc.
432 Park Avenue South, Suite 1503
New York, NY 10016, USA

British Library Cataloguing in Publication Data

Lloyd Thomas, David
    In defence of Liberalism.
    1. Liberalism
    I. Title
    320.5'1   JC571

    ISBN 0–631–15964–9

Library of Congress Cataloging in Publication Data

Lloyd Thomas, David.
    In defense of liberalism.
    Includes index.
    1. Liberalism. 2. Right of property. I. Title.
    JC585.L55   1988   320.5'1   87–31481

    ISBN 0–631–15964–9

Typeset in 11½ on 13 pt Times
by Cambrian Typesetters, Frimley, Surrey
Printed in Great Britain by
TJ Press, Padstow

Contents

Preface

One of the most disturbing things about books on political philosophy is that their authors are apt to present arguments for positions they believe in. One does not find an author of socialist persuasion explaining how (disconcerting though this was) he found himself led by reason to the conclusion that the rights of private property must be upheld come what may. The conclusions of books on political philosophy are apt to turn out surprisingly congenial to the political dispositions of their authors, given that they are supposed to be based on considerations that any reasonable person could accept.

The cynic may conclude that the real basis of political conviction lies in established dispositions. The formation of these dispositions would appear to depend on many contingencies: personal temperament, one's associates in formative years, the political context in which one's generation grew up, and the current outlook and interests of one's social group. Little in such dispositions may be owed to efforts at rational persuasion. The advocacy of various political theories then appears to be an intellectual epiphenomenon: an activity grounded in the desire to present a respectable intellectual front to one's adversaries. This book is written in the faith that the cynical view is not true, anyway of everyone and all the time. I do not know how the cynic could be disproved. How would we decide how much of a person's beliefs is attributable to dispositions which reasonable considerations neither formed nor now influence? Most of the conclusions of this book I find congenial. I would have more confidence that what is said is true if my inclination to believe it were less.

Liberals are occasionally called 'wishy-washy'. Sometimes this is a remark about the typical liberal temperament, as contracted with the 'tough' characters of fascism, Thatcherite conservatism and the militant left; in which case it is not, perhaps, too disturbing to be thought 'wishy-washy'. But the term can also be used as intellectual disparagement, to suggest that liberal theory is makeshift compromise. If one were rigorous and consistent, it seems to be suggested, one would be led to conclusions of the extreme right (or left). Regrettably this view is lent some encouragement by Hobbes's *Leviathan*: 'extremist' and probably the most rigorous piece of political theorizing we have. I hope to show, however, that the adoption of extreme political views is no guarantee of the rigour of one's thought, and that moderation is no proof of its absence.

Many people have helped to criticize, shape and develop the ideas in this book since they were first presented to the Department of Philosophy's Graduate Seminar at the University of North Carolina at Chapel Hill in May 1982. I am very grateful to those who contributed to the most helpful discussion on that occasion, especially Stephen Darwall; and since then, for similar favours, to John Charvet and the Graduate Seminar in Political Philosophy at the London School of Economics; to John Watkins and David-Hillel Ruben and the Department of Philosophy Graduate Seminar, also at the London School of Economics; to my colleagues at a King's College Department of Philosophy Staff Seminar; to Cyril Barrett and the University of Warwick Department of Philosophy Conference; to Hillel Steiner and the Postgraduate Seminar in the Department of Government at the University of Manchester; to Andrew Melnyk and the Hayek Society of Oxford; and to David Conway and the Philosophy Society at Middlesex Polytechnic.

My thanks are also due to those philosophy students at the University of London with whom these ideas have been discussed for the past several years. Bruce Landesman attended lectures at which an earlier version of some of this material was presented and kindly supplied me with his written comments. For more than two decades John McCloskey has been a continuing source of encouragement of my efforts to write on political philosophy. My thanks are due to King's College London for a term's leave during which the final draft was written, and to my colleagues who covered for me during my absence. Kendal Anderson produced an elegant final typescript with speed and efficiency.

I am grateful to the Aristotelian Society for permission to reproduce two short passages from my contribution to the symposium 'Liberty, Equality, Property' in *Proceedings of the Aristotelian Society*, Supplementary Volume LV, 1981.

The influence of Jerry Cohen on the development of my ideas can be gauged from the frequent references. He has commented on most of the text in various versions with a stimulating combination of sharp and precise criticism and unflagging encouragement of my attempts to develop my ideas and see them into print. It may not be entirely to his liking to be praised for liberal virtues, but I know of no one more committed to the pursuit of the truth, wheresoever that might lead.

I owe most to Anne Lloyd Thomas. She has been involved in every aspect of writing this book, from the discussion of embryonic ideas to the preparation of the final draft. Her inexhaustible emotional and intellectual support has been as indispensable to this as to anything else I have attempted to do. It is to her that the book is dedicated.

D. A. Lloyd Thomas
London

1

What Liberalism Is

Liberals attempt to justify a framework of legal and social requirements within which many styles of life and conceptions of what is worth while may be pursued. Liberals wish to present this as a 'neutral' framework, not biased towards any particular conception of what is worth while. But they also want to say that it is, in some clear sense, the *best* framework to have: frameworks which are non-liberal are also worse ones. The dilemma for liberals is to explain how both of these claims can be true. For if the liberal framework is the best-justified one, presumably it is best in terms of some conception of what is good; and that is, after all, to take some specific stand on what is good or worth while.

One response to this problem is to say that the neutral framework is not justified by reference to any conception of what is good. The justification for the neutral framework is deontological: 'the concept of right is prior to that of the good'.[1] But deontological justifications do not avoid taking a view about what is good. Certainly, they avoid making an appeal to good consequences, but they do not avoid making an appeal to a conception of what is good, and then using it in a non-consequentialist way. For example, it has to be assumed that a person's rational nature is something valuable if this is to serve as any kind of justification for persons being treated as ends in themselves.

My proposal for the defence of liberalism returns to consequentialist justifications, but to an eccentric form of consequentialism. The neutral framework indeed is justified by reference to something we consider to be good, but it is something that is good from the point of view of everyone; namely, having better-founded views about what is worth while in itself. Thus the neutral framework is justified in terms of something it is reasonable for everyone to consider good, and yet is not biased towards any particular conception of what is good. The idea could be put in pseudo-Kantian terminology by saying that the justification of the neutral framework follows from the concept of something's being of value in itself, not from any particular view of what is of value. Such a justification for liberalism is, in a sense, consequentialist; but it is not a conventional maximizing form of consequentialism. One respect in which it differs from conventional forms of consequentialism is that it is not presupposed (as it is in classical utilitarianism) that we know what is good. The attempt to discover what is worth while depends on experimentation with different 'modes of existence', a process which can best take place within the neutral framework.

Rights of self-ownership

It is necessary to give a characterisation of this neutral framework. The literature does not offer us a generally accepted, reasonably precise account. We have more confidence in recognising people of liberal temperament than in proposing a schematic account of the tenets of liberalism. We might start with examples of reactions and attitudes which would generally be agreed to be liberal. 'You shouldn't cut off her allowance because she has changed from law to philosophy. I know it's not what you wanted for her, but it's for her to decide.' 'Academic life was impossible under Stalin: no one could dispute an official line.' 'No law making homosexual acts between consenting adults an offence ought to be enacted.' 'Universities are not training institutions for meeting the demands of the economy.' 'You should not shout down speakers you disagree with.'

The common element in this collection of attitudes is a concern for freedom, of an individual or a group. That from which freedom is sought differs: parental pressure, dogmatic dictatorship, illegality, philistine government policy and silencing behaviour; and that which it is desired people should be free to do varies similarly. As a first attempt, then, at characterising liberalism more tightly, we might devise a list of liberal freedoms. One such list is given by J. S. Mill: liberty of thought and feeling, freedom of opinion and sentiment on all subjects, the liberty of expressing and publishing opinions, liberty to frame the plan of our life to suit our own character, and freedom to unite for any purpose not involving harm to others.[2] A somewhat different set of freedoms is to be found in Rawls: political liberty (the right to vote and to be eligible for public office), freedom of speech and assembly, liberty of conscience and freedom of thought, freedom of the person, the right to hold (personal) property, and freedom from arbitrary arrest and seizure.[3] It will be noticed that Rawls's list has a more 'political' tone than Mill's. It will not be assumed that a list of freedoms characteristic of a liberal temperament has relevance only in the context of law and politics: some of these freedoms may be infringed in the intolerant or dictactorial behaviour of some individuals or groups towards others.

It might be possible to narrow differences between the two lists in various ways: for example, by eliminating those from Rawls's list, such as the right to vote and to be eligible for public office, which are characteristic freedoms of democracy, not liberalism. There is, however, another approach to introducing a greater coherence into a formulation of liberalism. We might speculate that the freedoms in question are grounded on a certain view of the rights persons have. It is a common, though not, of course, a unique way of showing that a person ought to be free to do a certain thing to show that there is a right which grounds that freedom. The daughter ought to be allowed to decide freely whom to marry because that is her right; and a person is free to spend her own money, that is, money over which she has rights.

The idea that an appropriate list of freedoms might be generated by considering what a defensible set of individual rights would entail is a thread running through the liberal tradition. It is apparent in Locke and Kant. At first sight it cannot be found in J. S. Mill, but a little probing shows that his 'one very simple principle' rests on a substructure of individual rights.[4] Let us then pursue the proposal that a liberal position rests upon a view of what the rights of individuals are, and that the defence of a characteristically liberal set of freedoms will be a defence of that ascription of rights.

Before considering the substance of such rights a comment is appropriate on their type. We are not thinking of a conception of rights of individuals derived from some extant legal system or set of social conventions. For obviously such systems and conventions vary from place to place and from time to time, but we are seeking a set of rights which any person may be claimed to possess. Furthermore, some systems and conventions (indeed, historically speaking, nearly all) do not take a view of the rights of individuals upon which a liberal set of freedoms could be based. For example, they may acknowledge no right on the part of individuals to dissent from established religion. And in any case to ground an account of such rights in extant legal systems and social conventions would be to put the cart before the horse, for the point of developing an account of liberal rights and freedoms is to provide an independent basis for the criticism of existing law and social convention.

It would now seem that the type of rights we are considering are 'natural' rights. The term 'natural rights' can be used in a weaker and in a stronger way. In the weaker sense it simply refers to the existence of rights which are not dependent on an extant legal system or social convention. It is in this sense that I am prepared to accept that the rights upon which the liberal freedoms are based are natural rights. The stronger sense of 'natural rights' makes not only the claim just mentioned, but as well a claim about how natural rights must be conceived: i.e. that there is some characteristic of each person such that possession of that characteristic implies that a person has a certain right. We may refer to this conception as 'perceived' natural rights because it is claimed that any rational person will be able to 'see' the connection between possession of the characteristic(s) and possession of the rights. This conception of natural rights is commonly (though questionably) attributed to Locke.

I do not believe that it is possible to justify any natural rights if they are construed as 'perceived' natural rights. If a right is understood as a perceived natural right, no claim about the consequences of assuming that persons possess such a right can be admitted into its justification. It has to be claimed that every person who has the right possesses a certain characteristic (or set of characteristics) such that it follows from their possessing that characteristic (or those characteristics) that they have the right. Kant proposes that, as persons are rational beings, they have the right to be treated as ends in themselves and not as means only.[5] However, the characteristic in question does not ground the right: it is possible to accept that persons are rational beings, but to deny that they have such a right. The same appears to be true of all other attempts to ground rights in this way.

However, there is another conception of rights which also has a good claim to the title 'natural' because it may be contrasted with rights conceived of as deriving from positive law or convention. These are rights we believe ought to be *assigned* to persons in view of certain general moral considerations, whether or not they in fact are assigned by positive law or social convention. It could be held, for example, that there ought to be rights of self-ownership because owning oneself allows one to exercise autonomous choice, and autonomous choice is something objectively morally desirable. Such rights are seen as assigned, i.e.

whether people have them is thought of as dependent on correct reasoning from general moral principles or claims. By contrast, those who regard natural rights as 'perceived' do not think that we assign natural rights in this way: rather, we are simply called upon to recognise them. (It is not, of course, suggested that in the case of assigned natural rights there is some person, or some group fo persons, acting in accordance with a decision procedure, who does the assigning.)

In the example just given of reasoning from general moral principles the basis of assignment was that certain rights would constitute an instantiation of autonomy; something held to be of moral value. But assigned natural rights might also be seen as derived from consequentialist moral considerations. For example, natural rights might be seen as related to justifiable practices. The requirements of a practice supply the connection between the characteristic(s) possessed by a person and the claim that he or she has a certain right. The justification of the practice requires a comparison of the consequences there would be if that practice existed with the consequences if alternative practices existed, the comparison to be made in terms of some end(s). (This way of justifying rights may be referred to as 'practice consequentialism'.) On this view the connection between characteristics possessed by persons and rights must be made through a practice consequentially justified, whereas the justification of 'perceived' natural rights does not require any reference to practices and their consequences.

We can also use the term 'assigned' for natural rights justified in the practice-consequentialist way. Persons are thought of as in an initial condition of lacking rights, and are then assigned rights on the basis of justified practices. A reluctance to allow that assigned natural rights really are natural rights is due perhaps to the belief that natural rights must be 'natural' in both of two ways. They should be 'natural' rather than 'artificial' in that they exist prior to the 'artificial' contrivances of positive law or human convention. (I agree that natural rights must be 'natural' in this sense.)

And they should be natural rather than artificial in the sense that no 'contrived' processes of reasoning are necessary for their attribution: they are simply properties people have. (I deny that natural rights must be 'natural' in this sense.)

An indication has now been given of the type of right required in a defence of liberalism: it is an 'assigned' natural right. But to say only this much leaves open what might be the content of such natural rights. We must now consider the substance of the liberal rights of the individual. One proposal is attractive because of its simplicity. It assigns only one right to each person, viz. 'Every person is assigned an equal right to engage in any activity he/she chooses, provided only that when engaging in any activity no other person is involved without that person's consent.' This proposal is superior to a close alternative in terms of non-coercion. 'Every person is assigned an equal right to engage in any activity he/she chooses provided only that no one is coerced into any activity.' The latter would allow people to engage others in their activities provided only that coercion was not involved, for example, making use of another's unconscious body.

This suggestion immediately raises a problem, however. Virtually anything we do involves some others in the sense that it impinges in some way on their desires, even if only their unimportant desires. So if involving others means affecting them in this fashion there would be little any one person could do without obtaining the consent of some, perhaps of many, others. This single, basic right of individuals would not, in that case, generate the usual freedoms we associate with liberalism. For example, exercising the freedom to associate with others well may affect third parties. If their consent to our association were required, however, little would remain of freedom of association.

The obvious solution to this difficulty is to say that one may not involve others without their consent when that involves something with respect to which those others have rights. But now our conception of what it is to involve others presupposes that we *already* have an account of what people's rights are. The original simple and supposedly basic right is not in fact basic after all: a prior account of what are the rights of individuals is presupposed.

We cannot, at this point, make use of a conception of rights of individuals derived from some extant legal system or other human convention, for the reasons already indicated. Nor can we make use of a hypothetical contract argument after the style of Rawls. For persons in the original position are presented as choosing between various conceptions of justice,[6] and that already assumes that each party in the original position has the right to make such a choice on his or her own behalf. I have no right to make your selection of a principle of justice on your behalf in the original position. In other words, some conception of rights of self-ownership is presupposed in Rawls's argument for the two principles of justice: and that conception cannot itself be defended by a hypothetical contract argument.

The most plausible set of rights to propose is rights of self-ownership. These are understood as the rights of each person to control his or her own thoughts, talents, capacities, actions and body. Your rights of control are limited in that they do not permit you to act in such a way as to violate the similar rights of control of another person. You may not hit another person without his consent, but you may hit yourself. As everyone is assigned rights of control in his or her own person, and not in anyone else, it follows that no one has an enforceable, non-contractual claim on the services of anyone else as of right. It could still be, of course, that you have moral obligations to render services to others, but if so, those obligations are not grounded on the rights of others, except in the case of an express contract.[7]

Rights of self-ownership share a feature with private-property rights: they are both 'rights of control'. Rights of control held by one person exclude others from making choices regarding the things over which the rights are held without the permission of that person. There is a clear analogy between the rights of control people have over their own persons and the rights of control owners of property have over what they own. In both cases the recognition of a right of control by P over O implies the exclusion of others from the right to control O. And in both cases, if we believe that a right of control exists we believe that legitimacy is conferred upon the situation arising from the exercise of the right. It is not suggested, however, that there is any simple argument from the acceptance of rights of control over one's person to the acceptance of that specific set of rights of control involved in the notion of private property. Indeed in chapter 4 it will be argued that the acceptance of rights of self-ownership for reasons appropriate for a liberal implies the rejection of 'strong' private-property rights. But rights of self-ownership and private-property rights are both instances of the same generic form of right, a 'right of control', and distinct from, for example, one's right not to be excluded from the use of a public beach: a right which gives no one control over the beach.

If we think of the rights a liberal is concerned to defend as rights of self-ownership, it is plausible that such a set of rights would generate a typical list of liberal freedoms. For example, your thoughts are yours, i.e. things over which you have rights of control. Therefore you have the right to decide what your thoughts shall be, not anyone else. Therefore you ought to enjoy freedom of thought. It is plausible that the other freedoms Mill mentions similarly would be implied by acceptance of the rights of self-ownership.

The freedoms I believe people ought to have are the ones they have when everyone's rights of self-ownership are respected. The idea that people have such rights is intuitively attractive to us. Much of what we believe ourselves to be legally and morally forbidden to do is what one would be forbidden to do if rights of self-ownership were respected. Further, we think of the *reasons* for which we are forbidden to do these things in terms of rights of self-ownership. Surgery without consent properly obtained is seen as an invasion of someone's sphere of control rather than, say, as imposing intolerable risks on someone. The attractiveness of such rights is, however, no reason for omitting a justification of them. It is only recently, in historical terms, that it has been accepted that all adults have such rights, even in the West.

We may note, first, that it is not possible to justify rights of self-ownership as 'perceived' natural rights. It is not possible to find some characteristic or set of characteristics of a person such that it follows that that person owns himself. Obviously the fact that a person can control his body and actions or can control them in a 'rational' way, does not entail that he has a right to do so. Nor does it follow from something being mine (i.e. part of me) that it is mine (i.e. that over which I have rights of control). I do not mean to deny that the fact that my arm is mine (part of my body) is a good reason for why I, not you, should control it. What I deny is that it is a good reason 'in isolation', without a background practice being assumed under which it becomes a good reason. We easily assume and accept such a practice, so it is for us an obviously good reason. But the practice nevertheless stands in need of justification.[8] It is true that if the ownership of a person P is considered to be vested in another person Z, then Z, in order to get P to do what Z wants, must 'work through' P's 'will'. But the same is true of a horse and its owner, and we do not, for this reason, think that horses have rights of self-ownership and cannot be owned by people.

If we compare the ownership of persons with the ownership of material things we are struck by this difference. If we imagine a situation in which there are several people and many as yet unowned useful material things, there is no very obvious way in which to connect a particular person with a particular material thing. (Certainly there is not if there has been no history of association between person P and object O. Suppose eight of us have just waded ashore from our life rafts onto an uninhabited and unclaimed island. Who owns what? Even if we believe that the correct way to divide things between us is to give each of us equally good shares, that does not tell us which particular thing a particular person is to have.) By contrast, if it is suggested that people are to do the owning of people, there is a very natural solution to the question of which person owns which. Suppose the members of a tribe think of themselves as owned by God, and each morning go to a place where God will, by certain signs, give instructions as to what each is to do that day. Then the members of the tribe come to believe that there is no God. So there is the question 'Now, who owns whom?'. A natural answer is to assign the ownership of each person to that person. There is no similar 'natural' answer in the case of unowned material things. But this point is not a conclusive argument for self-ownership rather than, say, ownership by a member of the tribe elected as a secular substitute for God, or each person having an equal share in the ownership of all persons in the tribe.

It is not plausible, then, that rights of self-ownership can be justified as 'perceived' natural rights. They must be regarded as 'assigned' natural rights. On what grounds can such an assignment be justified? Not on the grounds that it maximizes freedom. One reason for this is that (as will be shown in chapter 2) it is not possibie to justify rights by any form of maximizing-consequentialist argument. Another reason, specific to the idea of a maximizing-consequentialist argument in terms of freedom, is that we have no clear conception of what it means to 'maximize freedom'.[9]

Consider, as an example,[10] a debate between (1) those who claim that freedom is maximized if all economic entitlements are determined by individual private-property rights alone, and (2) those who maintain that it is maximized if exchanges between property owners are subject to an 'equality rule' which says that no one is to have less than a certain amount below, or more than a certain amount above, the average level of holdings. Let us adopt MacCallum's analysis of freedom as a triadic relation.[11] Some person or agent, P, is free from R (some constraint, restriction, interference, or barrier) to do A (normally, some action). The understanding of R is taken widely: it may cover moral requirements, legal restrictions, external force, threats, lack of awareness, false consciousness, and strong desires and compulsions. Expressing the issue in terms of this analysis, we have the following package of freedoms and absences of freedom under a pure-ownership system.

1 All are free from some particular kind of restraint R (legal) to determine the next owner of what any one of them owns.
2 It is possible that some are not free from R to exercise rights of control over any holdings.

If the 'equality rule' holds then:

3 It is not the case that all are free from R to determine who next shall exercise rights of control over the holdings he now has.
4 All are free from R to exercise rights of control over some, at least minimal, set of holdings.

As different kinds of freedom are involved, it is unclear that any conclusion can be reached about which situation is preferable from the point of view of 'maximum' freedom. The only case where it is clear that a greater or lesser freedom exists is where the class of persons and the kind of restriction remains constant, but the extent of what a person is free to do is increased or decreased. If, at t_1 P is free from legal restraint to exercise rights of control over O_1 (and only O_1), and at t_2 P is free from legal restraint to exercise the same set of rights of control over O_1 and O_2 P has a more extensive freedom than at t_1, this situation being considered in isolation. Thus while my defence of liberalism will be a defence of self-ownership and the freedoms of individuals which follow from that idea[12] it will not be a defence in terms of 'maximizing freedom'. A distinctively liberal defence will be developed in chapter 3.

Some further refinement of this approach to characterising liberalism in terms of rights of self-ownership is necessary. Not all violations of these rights would ordinarily be thought to raise distinctively liberal considerations; murder, torture, kidnap, and rape as perpetrated by ordinary criminals are not usually thought of as distinctively liberal issues. (Though when these acts are the instruments of a repressive regime, such violations of people's rights assume a more distinctively liberal complexion.) It is a certain *range* of violations of rights of self-ownership a liberal is particularly concerned to oppose: lack of freedom of speech, publication, assembly, movement, and style of life; and the grosser (criminal) violations of rights of self-ownership when they are employed in the attempt to deny such freedoms.

A liberal not only focuses on a particular range of violations of the rights of self-ownership, however, but also is concerned about those violations for a certain kind of reason. It is possible to propose equal respect for rights of self-ownership for reasons which do not have a distinctively liberal character. For example, in a period of civil strife due to religious intolerance, 'equal respect for rights of self-ownership might be proposed as the basis of a *modus vivendi*. This may indeed be a sound reason for proposing such rights, given that it is likely that the proposal will be accepted generally, but it is not a characteristically liberal reason. The concern is social peace and stability, and the rights are seen as desirable only in so far as they serve this end: an end not itself distinctively liberal. A distinctively liberal reason is the relationship between the maintenance of those rights and the discovery of the truth. Truth on any matter is involved here: the truth in the natural or social sciences, in religion, in history, and in the conduct of government. My concern will be with one particular area in which the truth is sought – the truth as to what is worth while in itself.

The liberal freedoms are related to concern for the truth, a concern which may be either intrinsic or instrumental. Characteristically a government, class, or other group which practises some form of injustice, repression, or exploitation has greater difficulty in doing so in an environment where the truth can be readily investigated, ascertained, and widely disseminated. Those who hate injustice have reason to love the liberal freedoms. The importance of this instrumental concern for the liberal freedoms is not, of course, denied: in some sense, perhaps, it is more fundamental than the concern I shall be advancing – the truth about what is worth while for its own sake. It is to be emphasised, therefore, that my defence of rights of self-ownership is *a*, not *the*, defence of those rights.

Liberal considerations as decisive

Having formulated liberalism in terms of a set of rights, it is quite natural to expect that liberal considerations will then be employed in a certain way in political debate. It is common for considerations brought forward in political debate to be widely acknowledged as relevant while their decisiveness is contested. For example, it is pointed out that the pursuit of a certain measure would have regrettable effects on the property rights of some, and this is allowed as relevant; but its conclusiveness as an objection to the measure is contested. As this is so endemic a feature of political debate, it is natural for political philosophers to seek out considerations which, when brought into play in the consideration of policies, decide upon their acceptance or rejection. Liberals have wished to make liberal considerations decisive in this way: they have sought to make the liberal freedoms rocks in the ebb and flow of other, more fluid, political considerations. In the liberal state the liberal rights and liberties of individuals are the basis of the constitutional structure. They form the categorical framework of the political union. Political and social goals may be pursued within that framework, but only to the extent that their pursuit is consistent with it. This view, endorsed by Mill and Rawls, gives priority to the liberal rights and liberties over other political considerations in all normal circumstances.[13]

However, liberal reasons for rights of self-ownership have been distinguished from reasons of other kinds. Could those distinctively liberal reasons be sufficient to give rights of self-ownership the decisive place claimed for them in the political structure? It is doubtful whether they could. But this does not imply that, after all, we must deny the priority of the rights and liberties of the liberal state. We must distinguish between the liberal state and liberal reasons for the liberal state. Liberal reasons or, anyway, my liberal reasons, do not alone provide a reason for making the liberal rights and liberties categorical. They are not categorical for this or perhaps any other single reason, but because of the combined weight of reasons of several different kinds, some not distinctively liberal in character. It is because respect for rights of self-ownership (and the consequent individual rights and liberties) has so many independent and weighty supports that it should serve as the basis of the constitutional structure of the state. Liberals have too readily supposed that if the requirements of the liberal state are to be categorical, then the distinctively liberal reasons for the liberal state must themselves be categorical.

The liberal rights and liberties are decisive, though their being decisive does not rest wholly on the liberal character of these considerations. But how can this view be maintained for every kind of political situation? Can it be maintained in wartime, or when there is revolution or severe political instability? Many kinds of case come up here, of which we may mention two. One is where a state generally committed to the liberal rights and liberties comes under threat, from internal violence or external military attack. Suppose the most, or only, effective way the state has of defending itself involves some violation of the liberal rights and liberties, such as restrictions on the political liberties of a certain section of the population. Would it not be plausible to relax the requirement that the liberal rights and liberties

are decisive? The other case is that of societies which might
be described as 'pre-liberal'. One example would be a
society in which the political structure is so fragile that there
often may be doubt about the capacity of a government to
enforce the law effectively, whether the law is liberal or
otherwise. Another case is where a society is so far from
realizing a liberal conception of people's rights and liberties
that it would be hopelessly idealistic to demand their
recognition, e.g. demanding the right to be a publicly
professed atheist in sixteenth-century Europe.

To deal with the problems raised by cases such as these we
need to distinguish two kinds of liberal commitment.
(A) Commitment to the goal of the liberal society; that is,
the society in which everyone's rights of self-ownership are
fully respected. (B) Commitment to a certain choice of
policy in a particular political situation. A commitment to
(A) is always appropriate, but it does not follow that the
best policy to commit oneself to under (B) is (A). For
example, in seventeenth-century England some limited
degree of religious toleration was a political possibility in
certain periods, but at no time was a degree of religious
toleration that would permit the public profession of
atheism possible. Now religious toleration that includes the
right to be an atheist is closer to the ideal liberal polity than
toleration without that right. But it does not follow that, if
committed to the ideal liberal polity, one should espouse the
broader, rather than the narrower, form of religious
toleration. For there was no political possibility at that time
of the broader form being accepted, whereas there sometimes was a good chance of the narrower form being
accepted. Therefore to have supported the broader form at
that time might only have had the effect of allowing religious
intolerance to prevail; something even further from the
liberal ideal than the narrower form of religious toleration.
The liberal freedoms are always justified, but the best policy
to adopt is sometimes something less than their complete
realisation.

Now generally in modern Western liberal democracies

liberal considerations are decisive. Of course sometimes arguments will be advanced that they should not be regarded as decisive in particular cases, because, if they were to be, the whole structure of the liberal state would be weakened. This form of argument must be allowed as legitimate, but in nearly all cases it will not be successful because there is no reason to believe that the continued universal recognition of the liberal rights and liberties poses any threat whatsoever to the structure of the liberal state. Suggestions that they should be compromised nearly always will be corrupt. Often the existence of the liberal freedoms does threaten powerful established interests, and those interests simply seek protection at the cost of the rights of others.

Concern that the liberal freedoms should be respected has normally had a particular object: it has been the grounds for claiming that the law ought to have a certain character. Indeed the way in which some of the liberal freedoms have been formulated has apparently presupposed that this is the sphere in which they are to have application. Freedom of expressing and publishing opinions and freedom of assembly would seem to assume this context; in that the state is seen both as a potential violator and, in the case of freedom of assembly, as the principal agent for the guarantee of this freedom. However, the force of the liberal set of rights and their implied freedoms extends to many more areas than those directly involving questions about what legislation should be. They can be relevant to other political matters, such as whether an illiberal law ought to be obeyed. And they apply to many areas which are not directly political at all. Parents may insufficiently respect the choices of their children as to what their 'plan of life' should be, curricula may be unduly restrictive on students' choices of areas of study, and a theatre company may take a narrow view of the type of play it is appropriate to produce. It is not my intention to follow through all of these applications, but to attempt a defence of the core of this outlook, the liberal rights and freedoms.

2
Rights and Maximizing Consequentialism

It is likely that a familiar set of liberal freedoms can be derived from rights of self-ownership. How are such rights to be justified? One approach is consequentialist: it is argued that good consequences would follow from the universal assignment of such a set of rights. In this chapter it will be argued that it is not possible to justify such a set of rights, or indeed any rights, on the basis of 'maximizing' consequentialism. In chapter 3 it will be shown that such rights can be justified on the basis of an unconventional form of consequentialism, to be called 'experimental' consequentialism.

For a consequentialist defence of a set of rights to be successful two things have to be established: (1) that there is good reason to suppose that consequences of a certain kind are good; and (2) that the right in question can be justified consequentially by reference to that supposition about what is good. There are difficulties for consequentialist theories with respect to (1), some of which will be raised in the second part of chapter 5, but they will not be pressed here. Attention will be given only to (2). It will be shown that no right (of whatever content) can be justified by the argument that it maximizes some good. It does not matter, for this demonstration, what the good is supposed to be.[1]

Consequentialist positions are usually divided into act and practice consequentialism. (Act and Rule Utilitarianism may be regarded as special cases of these more inclusive positions.) Act consequentialism holds that that act is right which, of the alternatives available, can be expected to have the best consequences from the point of view of maximizing the occurrence of some good(s). Now if a person has a certain right he may be regarded as enjoying the protection of a 'barrier' which normally protects the possessor of the right from being treated in ways which might be justified in terms of the advantages to everyone concerned of so treating him. For example, if you own a book, you have the right to decide what is to be done with it. The fact that there would be better consequences for all concerned if your decisions were ignored does not normally count as a reason for ignoring them, if those decisions are seen as protected by your rights. But if you are an act consequentialist you cannot consistently assert that there are some categories of act which are protected from reasoning about what would be the optimal consequences. For this reason one cannot hope for an act-consequentialist justification of the rights of individuals.

Practice consequentialism appears to hold out better prospects for justifying the rights of individuals. The practice-consequentialist view is that respect for a right, *R*, in a particular situation, is justified by reference to a practice, *P*, which confers *R* on such a person in such a situation. Acceptance of what *P* requires, as against what other possible practices would require, is justified by showing that *P* will have the most acceptable consequences from the point of view of maximizing some good.

One difficulty with a practice-consequentialist attempt to justify rights is apparent from the following illustration. Suppose private property is held to be a consequentially justified practice, and possession by someone of ownership rights over something is taken to include the owner's having the right to destroy it if he chooses. In a particular case upholding ownership rights so understood is found to have worse consequences (in terms of the good adopted) than ignoring it. It would seem that the practice consequentialist should propose a modified practice, such as private-property rights with restrictions on the right to destroy, which would produce the best consequences in this particular case. But if the practice consequentialist does allow a modification in any instance when to do so would secure better consequences than adhering to the original view of what the practice should be, then any supposed right is liable to continuous revision and erosion. In effect rights are no better secured than they would be by an act-consequentialist justification. But if, for these reasons, the practice consequentialist does not allow modifications of proposed practices, it appears that he must regard consider-ations other than consequentialist ones as relevant to the justification of practices.

So it seems that practice consequentialism fails to offer a satisfactory defence of rights of individuals. Why? It conceives of the relationship between a justified practice, assigning rights to individuals, and the occurrence of what is held to be good, as one of *maximization*. A given right R is held to be justified only if the consequences of a practice incorporating R maximize the bringing about of the end selected as good. So long as the relationship is one of maximization, the optimal practice, and hence the justified set of rights, must be open to revision whenever there is a change in the contingent circumstances affecting the likely consequences of a given practice.

To this argument the following objection may be made.[2] My argument would appear to assume the following. Suppose that there is a generally accepted practice P, and that in certain circumstances C it would be best to do A, which is forbidden by P. There is an alternative, but similar, practice P_1, such that under P_1 it would be required or permissible to do A. I appear to be assuming that the practice consequentialist must shift allegiance from P to P_1. But the practice consequentialist does not necessarily have to shift allegiance from P to P_1. For although P_1 may have better consequencies in circumstances C than P, it does not follow that overall the consequences of following P_1 would be better than those of following P, or, more interestingly, that there will be any other practice which will have better consequences than following P.

In reply it may be said that surely it must be a possibility that there should be cases where it is better for the practice consequentialist to shift allegiance from P to some other practice P_n, even when everything about acting in accordance with the alternative practice has been taken into account. Would this not erode any confidence in rights justified in a practice-consequentialist fashion? In reply to this the practice consequentialist can bring in two further considerations.

1 Though possible that there should be some such alternative practice P_n, it may be in fact very unlikely that there is one.
2 But even supposing that there is a practice P_n apparently superior overall to P, which accommodates doing A in circumstances C, there is a further consideration against switching allegiance to P_n. An aspect of the good produced by P depends on people's security of expectation that P will be followed. Taking this good into account as well, it may be best to stick with it.

But even taking this further factor into consideration, a practice consequentialist presumably must allow that there could be some cases in which allegiance should be changed to P_n, i.e. cases in which the expected gains in switching to P_n outweigh the loss due to the disappointment of people's expectations that P would be followed. The question would then be whether, on such a justification of practices, we would have rights which could be regarded as sufficiently secure. (The practice consequentialist could not show that they would be completely secure, but it is assumed that this does not have to be shown, as no reasonable advocate of rights would wish to claim that they are.)

In any case there is a more general argument to show why rights cannot be justified by maximizing-consequentialist arguments. Consider one difference between these moral requirements.

1 You ought to get Sally to hospital at once.
2 You ought to leave Sally's things alone.

The first requires that, of all the things you might choose to do, you are to do *this* thing. The second does not indicate which of all the things you might choose to do you should choose. It only requires that, out of your set of possible choices, you do *not* make certain ones, namely, messing about with Sally's things. We may divide moral requirements into those which direct that, from your set of possible choices, you make this or that specific choice, and those which do not. The latter go no further than to indicate that you do not make certain choices, and leave it to you to decide which of the remaining choices you do make. Claims that individuals have certain rights are normally of the latter kind. To say that Sally has the right to choose what to do with her things is not to say either what choice she ought to make, or what choice you ought to make. It is only to say that there is a certain set of choices it is permissible for her to make, and a certain set of choices it is not permissible for you to make.

It is not claimed that this is true of every use of the term 'right'. Perhaps Sally could say she has a right to expect that her sister would try to get her to hospital if she suddenly became ill. There are also cases where someone has the right to direct you to do this precise thing because you made an agreement to accept their direction. But it is true of the notion of a right which interests liberals. To have freedom of speech is to have the right to say what one thinks. Respect for one's rights to free speech does not require that one should choose to say certain things or that others should choose to say certain things. It only renders impermissible certain choices others could make, such as trying to silence you. It is compatible with this to allow that there are certain things it would be within one's rights to say which it would be morally objectionable to say. Respect for rights is only one form of moral requirement to which one is subject. Now the objective of a consequentialist-maximizing principle is to indicate which choice, from your set of possible choices, is the one you should make. To be sure, the application of a consequentialist-maximizing principle will not always be successful in attaining this objective. Insufficient information may leave indeterminate which of some narrowed-down set of choices is the one to be made. But the objective of a maximizing-consequentialist principle is, nevertheless, to indicate the precise choice to be made. Therefore those moral requirements, such as respect for the liberal rights of individuals, which do not attempt to indicate which choice a person should make, could not be justified by maximizing-consequentialist arguments.

As this argument against a maximizing-consequentialist defence of rights depends on the structure of moral requirements involving rights, and not on the content of those rights, it holds no matter what view is taken of the content of individual rights. In this respect it is superior to those arguments against consequentialist accounts of rights which presuppose that we know individuals to have rights with a certain content. For example, it might be said that every person has a right that society should provide him with minimal subsistence if he is unable to provide it for himself. It is then shown that if one accepts the principle of utility, there could be circumstances in which it was not optimal to provide everyone with minimal subsistence. This argument simply assumes that we know that there is such a right, and invites the utilitarian to ask why it should be supposed that we know that this is so. My argument, by contrast, need make no claim to know what rights people have, but only that people have rights (of a yet-to-be-determined content).

This argument against maximizing-consequentialist accounts of rights also holds irrespective of the kind of consequence held to be good, i.e. irrespective of whether it is happiness, desire-satisfaction, etc. Take, for example, a maximand apparently particularly unfavourable for my argument: the power of persons, in aggregate, to choose for themselves.[3] Even if this were the maximand, there could be reason to overturn certain rights – for example, the right of a person to choose whether others will have access to his body. If one were concerned to maximize the power of persons to choose, one could have reason to restrict the right of persons to choose who should have access to their bodies in certain cases. For example, a simple operation, using standard procedures, is necessary to save a young adult's life. There is a high probability of success, but the patient refuses consent. The restriction on the patient's right to choose would be much more than compensated for by preserving the patient's power to choose for the rest of a normal life.

There is a further argument against attempts to justify rights on the basis of maximizing-consequentialist consider-ations. The claim that all persons have a certain right (say, the right not to be tortured) may be represented as the claim that in the set of possible choices each person has, certain choices are impermissible. Now it is possible that, by reference to a certain maximizing-consequentialist criterion (such as the principle of utility), and given certain assump-tions about the empirical context, every choice ruled out by the requirement that the right be respected is also ruled out by the consequentialist criterion, because in every case that choice would not be optimal. Would this show that one had consequentialist reasons for respecting the right in question? It would show that, as a consequentialist, one ought to avoid all those choices that those who believe that there is a right believe you ought to avoid. But although the two positions would be the same in substance, it would not show that the consequentialist believes that people have that right. For the consequentialist must be prepared to 'violate' the right if the contingent circumstances were to change in an appropriate way, even if it is very unlikely that they would so change. Whereas one who believes that there is a right will not be prepared to violate the right in these circumstances.

'Realistic' consequentialism

The foregoing argument against a maximizing-consequentialist justification of rights may, however, be thought to be inconclusive because the form of consequentialism considered was too unsophisticated. (As the new form of consequentialism now to be considered does not depend essentially on the character of the maximand, let us call that 'utility', where 'utility' is regarded as a place-holder for any suitable maximand.) The departure point for this new form of consequentialism is an observation about the structure of the form of consequentialism we have just rejected as unable to supply a basis for rights. It has been assumed that if a practice P would be best for maximizing utility, then everyone (or a sufficient proportion of people to make P viable) will conform to P. But why should it be supposed that this will always be so? For example, it may be true that, in a poor Latin American country, it would be best for maximizing utility for the practice of using contraceptives to be adopted by sexually active women of child-bearing age. But if most of those women would not depart from the teachings of the Catholic Church on these matters, it would be absurd for a consequentialist to propose this practice, as few would comply with it.

The general point is that a consequentialist should not ask 'What is the best practice for promoting utility?' (it being assumed that whatever practice that is, nearly everyone will conform to it). Rather the question should be 'What is the best practice for promoting utility amongst the set of practices we reasonably could assume that the appropriate group of people would conform to?' If a practice is to produce utility, it must be a practice most people will follow. Practices hardly anyone follows will not yield the good results it was envisaged that the practice would have. A consequentialist will not be concerned with hypothetical gains in utility, but with actual ones, and these will flow only from practices most people do in fact follow.

We might then propose a new form of consequentialism, which may be called 'realistic' consequentialism. It would recommend that we proceed as follows. We take the set of possible practices (neglecting the question of to what degree they in fact would be complied with if it were attempted to put them into operation) and rank them in order of the amount of utility each could be expected to produce if everyone were to comply with each of them in turn. Then, starting with the best, we accept it if it would be reasonable to suppose that it would be generally complied with, reject it if not. If rejected, we turn to the next best, and so on, until we arrive at a practice it would be reasonable to expect would meet with general compliance.

If this procedure were followed for arriving at acceptable practices, it could be expected that those practices would reveal certain regular patterns. One of the patterns to emerge would be due to the fact that people are, to a considerable degree (though not entirely), self-regarding. Most people are unlikely to comply with a practice if it could call for considerable sacrifice of their own interests, as would be the case, for example, with the practice of commandeering bodily parts for transplants when necessary to save life.[4] Now those who ask that account be taken of the rights of individuals are in effect requiring that limits should be set on what degree of sacrifice can be demanded of the interests of any individual in order to maximize utility. This requirement can be met by realistic consequentialism. For practices which make excessive demands on the interests of individuals would not be viable, and so would have to be rejected. The remaining 'acceptable' practices would, *de facto*, contain no requirements we could consider contrary to people's rights.

This attempt to reinstate a basis for rights in a maximizing-consequentialist theory is open to a number of objections. I shall first mention two it is not my intention to press. Then I shall come to one which is, I think, a conclusive reason for rejecting this variant of consequentialism.

Realistic consequentialism says that the implications of an acceptable practice for individuals will not be so intolerable as to cause the practice not to gain general compliance. Now one of the things that makes the implications of a practice intolerable is the impact it would have on the existing moral beliefs of a community. If it is believed to be morally unacceptable to eat cows, then the implications of a practice requiring one to eat cows will be regarded as intolerable. Realistic consequentialism would seem to have to take into account such reasons for regarding moral practices as intolerable, for these considerations may make a proposed practice inoperative just as much as the strength of self-regarding dispositions. It follows that realistic consequentialism may generate an at least partially relativistic account of the rights people have.

More disturbing is a second objection based on the observation that a practice, in order to be viable, does not require that all of those subject to it will be prepared to conform to it. The willingness of a substantial majority to comply with its requirements on most occasions will be sufficient for a practice to be viable. (It would be pointless to attempt to specify the precise proportion complying that is required for this.) Thus it could be that a practice *P* is viable, despite the fact that from the point of view of a sufficiently small minority, its requirements are intolerable. Assuming that in some cases where individuals find the implications of a practice intolerable, their rights indeed are violated, it follows that this approach need not secure the rights of everybody, but only of a sufficiently large majority to ensure that the practice is viable. Realistic consequentialism does not rule out those practices that would affect everyone's interests too adversely, but only those that would adversely affect the interests of too large a number for the practice to be viable.

This problem would be met if it were specified that for a practice to be acceptable, its implications must be tolerable from the point of view of everyone subject to it. Such a requirement is implicit in Scanlon's version of consequentialism. 'An act is wrong if its performance under the circumstances would be disallowed by any system of rules for the general regulation of behaviour which no one could reasonably reject as a basis for informed, unforced general agreement.'[5] But the introduction of such a requirement would be arbitrary in the context of a purely consequentialist theory. At best it could be introduced into a consequentialist theory as a derivative test of the acceptability of a practice. But, as has been argued, it is not in fact necessary on purely consequentialist grounds that the test of acceptability should be strictly universal in the way that Scanlon's contract ground is.

We now come to the objection which makes realistic consequentialism unacceptable, at least from the point of view of a liberal conception of rights. The form of consequentialism now before us says that we are obliged to conform to the requirements of a practice P so long as P is the practice out of the set of viable practices which maximizes utility. Even if this account of our obligations does not call upon us to make substantial sacrifices of our interests, it is still implausibly stringent. People commit themselves to certain major projects which they see as giving their lives overall shape; such as rearing families, cultivating certain relationships, pursuing certain vocations and causes, and following certain leisure pursuits. Realistic consequentialism allows individuals no moral 'space' for these projects: our attempts to pursue them could always be interrupted by supposed moral demands grounded in the maximization of utility.[6] So even if this form of consequentialism could provide the basis for some individual rights (and even in this respect doubts have already been suggested), it could not provide grounds for a certain right which is especially important from a liberal point of view: the right of individuals to choose major projects in their lives for themselves, and to act in ways appropriate in relation to the pursuit of those projects. It may be true that in certain cultures (that of the contemporary West perhaps among them) the expectation that people will be allowed to make such choices for themselves is so strong as to render a contrary practice not viable. But this would make the status of such a right a fortuitous contingency. Such an expectation has not been widespread in most cultures.

The argument of this chapter has attempted to establish that it is not possible to justify a suitable set of rights for defending liberalism on the basis of maximizing-consequentialist arguments. This does not, however, eliminate the possibility of defending a suitable set of rights on the basis of non-maximizing-consequentialist arguments. It is to that possibility that I now turn.

3
Experimental Consequentialism

It has been argued that a defence of individual rights is not possible on the basis of maximizing consequentialism. Nevertheless it may still be possible to erect a consequentialist defence of the rights of individuals. For the fault so far identified in attempts at a consequentialist defence of rights does not lie simply in their being consequentialist, but in the assumption that the securing of the end held to be good must be maximized. There is no obvious reason why the relationship must be conceived of in terms of maximization. We can arrive at an alternative proposal through considering two examples where the relationship between rights and consequences is not that of maximization.

Those who appreciate football believe that sometimes sequences of play are good; good in the sense of 'intrinsically good': these episodes are to be admired for their own sake. Now the rules of the game may be regarded as assigning certain 'rights' to the players; for example, rights that certain forms of violence should not be practised upon them. Respect for this set of rights and the occurrence of good play are connected. It would not be possible to have the sequences of play thought to be good unless these rules were generally respected. But observance of the rules is not justified on the ground that it maximizes good play. The rules may be observed and yet no sequences of good play may occur, say, because the players are not sufficiently skilful.

Friendship serves as another example. It is widely regarded as rewarding and worth while for its own sake, and not just because, say, having connections can be useful. Now the existence of friendship is dependent on presumptions about the rights people have – in particular, the right to associate with others on the basis of inclination. But the connection between rights and what is valuable about friendship is not that those rights maximize what is valuable about friendship. People may enjoy the appropriate rights, but not make any rewarding friendships because, say, they are too self-preoccupied.

It may be objected, however, that the assignment of these rights does, on the whole, maximize the rewards of friendship, even if it is true that some people may enjoy these rights, but not make any rewarding friendships.[1]

It may be allowed that the universal assignment of a right to associate with any other person on the basis of inclination can be expected to maximize the rewards of friendship relative to certain other possibilities. Imagine, first, society *A* in which (1) there are certain others with whom one is obliged to associate irrespective of inclination and (2), regarding everyone else, one is obliged not to associate, even if one is inclined to. In such a society there still may be some friendships, because some people may ignore what are regarded as their obligations. It could not be, though, that friendship was very common, for if it were we would doubt whether rules (1) and (2) really were operative in that society.

Now imagine society *B* in which members of the upper class may associate with other members of the upper class on the basis of inclination, and similarly for members of the lower class; but no member of the upper class may associate with any member of the lower class on the basis of inclination. One would expect the rewards of friendship to be commoner in society *B* than in society *A*. If we now take society *C*, in which any member can associate with any other on the basis of inclination, it would be reasonable to expect that this right (the one liberals have in mind) would, relative to societies *A* and *B*, maximize the rewards of friendship.

Nevertheless it seems that a policy of maximizing the rewards of friendship is different from the universal assignment of a right to associate on the basis of inclination. Suppose psychological research showed that rewarding friendships are made only between persons who fall within the same personality category. However, persons not falling within the same category are often mutually attracted, though in these cases rewarding friendships never develop. In order to prevent people wasting time on such relationships someone concerned to maximize the rewards of friendship might propose limiting the rights of persons to associate with others on the basis of inclination to those in the same personality category. So the universal assignment of a right to associate with any other person on the basis of inclination might not maximize the rewards of friendship. There is a difference, then, between arguing for the universal right of association on the grounds that it is a precondition for the existence of friendship, and that it maximizes the rewards of friendship, even if, given our present knowledge, it is in fact reasonable to believe that such an assignment of rights does maximize the rewards of friendship.

As will be apparent shortly, my argument for the assignment of rights of self-ownership will not be that they tend to promote any particular conception of what is worth while, such as friendship.

The examples of football and friendship suggest the following idea. It is a condition for the existence of what is believed to be good about certain activities that certain rights, appropriate for participants in those activities, should be respected. This is a consequentialist justification of those rights: the case for the rights rests on creating the possibility that something worth while should exist. But this is not a maximizing-consequentialist justification, for the recognition of the appropriate rights only makes possible those activities that may be worth while.

So far no explanation has been given of what is meant by

saying that a certain right is a condition for the existence of
some particular form of goodness. Clearly it cannot mean
that recognition of the right is a necessary condition for the
occurrence of that form of goodness. In a society in which all
personal relationships were supposed to be either
mandatory or forbidden, some friendships no doubt would
occur.

To answer this question it is necessary to sketch a view of
the relationship between the good and self-interest. Judgements of intrinsic goodness are not conditional upon taking
up the standpoint of this or that person's interest. If
Mozart's version of *Don Giovanni* contains to a considerable degree elements of what is good in opera, it does so
irrespective of whether this fact is pleasing or displeasing to
Salieri. To have an egotistical reason for wanting something
non-instrumentally presupposes that there are available
judgements of intrinsic goodness *not* made from the point of
view of the interests of this or that person. Why want
something non-instrumentally unless you believe it to be
good apart from the fact that you happen to want it? This is
not to say that egotism presupposes altruism. Altruism is
concerned with desiring that the desires of others for what
they believe to be good are satisfied. One can believe that
something is intrinsically good without caring whether the
desires of others for it are satisfied. Indeed we might not
care whether our own desires for it are satisfied, because we
select for pursuit only some of the things we believe to be
intrinsically good. Even if, in believing that something is
good, we must in some sense desire it, it is not necessary
that we desire it as an end of action, for we may think that
we are in circumstances where it is inappropriate for us to
make it an end of action.

Wanting something for oneself (non-instrumentally) presupposes a judgement of intrinsic goodness not made from
the point of view of the interests of any particular person.
But this does not imply that one is motivated by exclusive
regard for the intrinsically good, and without regard for
what effect so acting may have on your own or another's

interests. A person's interest in what he believes to be intrinsically good is normally a self-preoccupied one. It is not suggested, however, that this self-preoccupation is in any way necessary, or even that people are invariably self-preoccupied.

Now we may return to the understanding to be given to the expression 'condition for' in my proposed version of consequentialism. To say that a given right R is a condition for the occurrence of something believed to be intrinsically good means that if self-interest were not restrained by general recognition of R, each person would tend to act in ways believed to be optimal for that person's self-interest, and the good in question would rarely occur. If every person violated a right respect for which is a condition for the existence of something believed to be intrinsically good (in order to try to have it for himself), then each would act in a self-defeating way. Their actions would prevent the existence of that which each sought to have.

It has been indicated how respect for a right of a certain kind might be justified on the ground that respect for the right is a condition for the existence of that which is believed to be good in a certain human activity. But how does this relate to the defence of a standard set of liberal rights? Here is one suggestion. There is a great variety of human activities each of which is thought by at least some people to contain possibilities of something worth while. Participants in each of these activities are presumed to have some set of rights which are conditions for the pursuit of that activity. Perhaps the rights of individuals a liberal seeks to defend represent what is *common* to all of these sets of rights.

There do indeed appear to be rights which are common to several activities, and are conditions for the pursuit of each of them. Examples would be the practice of history and philosophy, both of which require (at least in any form recognisable to us) the assumption that participants in them have the right to communicate with others engaged in the same activity. Nevertheless this idea cannot be used to defend a suitable set of individual rights for liberalism.

Often some people believe that something of value is to be found in a certain activity, while others fail to see this: they may think the activity worthless, or even repulsive or evil. An example would be monastic forms of life, regarded by some as worthless, and a waste of people's lives. Thus while certain believers may think there is reason for respecting those rights that are a condition for the pursuit of a monastic way of life, others may see no reason for respecting them. Indeed the conflict may be sharper than this. For example, a believer may regard the pursuit of scientific enquiry as likely to subvert religious faith, and see reason for denying or qualifying those rights that are the conditions for the pursuit of scientific enquiry.

Another way of approaching this point is by way of considering the moral requirements people are prepared to accept. The justification of some moral requirements would seem to depend on the acceptance, by those who see themselves as subject to them, that certain activities contain something of worth or value. Consider a commitment to 'intellectual honesty'. This I take to include a willingness to accept certain restraints in intellectual life, such as not publicly covering up private doubts about one's views, or the strength of the evidence for them, not espousing beliefs more because they support desired conclusions or favoured causes than because of one's confidence in their truth, refraining from 'intellectual bullying', etc. The acceptance of these restraints is, in one sense at least, optional. The virtue is appropriate only if one adopts certain interests or roles: it is not clear that an army officer, say, (*qua* army officer) can be, or fail to be, intellectually honest. (He can fail to face the realities of his military position, but that is different from being intellectually dishonest.) The acceptance of the moral restraints imposed by intellectual honesty depends on how they relate to certain objectives, such as truth and enlightenment, held to be desirable by those who have intellectual interests. It can, perhaps, be shown that there is an 'objective' relationship between the virtue of intellectual honesty and those aspirations, but it is not morally required that any particular person should have those aspirations. (It is not, of course, claimed that this is true of all moral requirements.) To sum up: any defence of a certain right which appeals to the claim that that right is a precondition for some particular thing held to be good by some person is hypothetical. It depends, for its success, on acceptance by others that that thing is worth while.

However, it is possible to defend liberal rights without having to assert that this or that particular human activity is valuable. How is it possible, though, that there should be a consequentialist defence of these rights unless some view is taken of what is good? My reply rests on the distinction between our beliefs about what activities are in fact intrinsically valuable, and what should be said about how we come to form more reasonable views about what activities are intrinsically valuable. The latter is a view about the method by which we come to have more reasonable views.

The case for a liberal set of individual rights does not rest on the assumption that we already know what is intrinsically valuable. Rather, it rests on a plausible claim about how it is possible to have better formed beliefs about what is valuable. The justification of such rights rests on what might be called an 'experimental' form of consequentialism. It differs from conventional consequentialism not only in that it is non-maximizing, but also in that it does not assume that we already know what is good: what is good is something to be discovered. This conception of consequentialism requires that people should be assigned rights which protect them from being prevented from engaging in activities they consider to be worth while, or from being forced into engaging in certain activities even when they do not think they are worth while. It is not denied, of course, that we have views about what activities are of value in themselves. But people differ on this question, and we cannot claim to have knowledge on these matters (though neither do I wish to say, as non-cognitivists do, that it is not possible that we should have knowledge). It would be contentious, therefore, to defend liberalism by appealing to some particular conception of what is valuable in itself.

In this respect the present defence of liberalism employs an unconventional conception of consequentialism. Normally a consequentialist view takes a stand on what constitutes good consequences (desire satisfaction, preference satisfaction, etc.). Though the present defence is consequentialist, it presupposes no particular view of what is desirable in itself. In avoiding such a presumption it has one advantage of a 'process' theory of individual rights, such as Nozick's entitlement theory.[2] The entitlement theory makes no assumptions about what is good or desirable: it does not need to suppose, for example, that it is good (either individually or collectively) for people to have more, rather than fewer, holdings. It attempts to say what rights to holdings individuals have independently of views about what are desirable ends. Similarly an experimental-consequentialist defence of individual rights does not require any assumption about what is of value, for the point of these rights is not that respect for them will tend to maximize the occurrence of some given conception of what is of value, but that they provide the basis for the discovery of what is of value. To avoid misunderstanding, it should be added that the present defence of liberalism does not entail an entitlement conception of rights of control over holdings: the point is simply that there is a theoretical similarity between that defence of liberalism and the entitlement theory in that they both defend certain (different) individual rights without having to take stands about what things are desirable as ends.

Here a sceptic concerning the possibility of knowledge of what is intrinsically good could point out that it is being assumed that we can have more or less reasonable beliefs about what is intrinsically good, even if we do not have knowledge. It is true that this is being assumed. We may distinguish between a weaker and a stronger scepticism concerning evaluative knowledge. The weaker scepticism says that we do not, as a matter of fact, know what things are intrinsically good. The stronger scepticism says that there could not be knowledge of what is intrinsically good. The weaker form of scepticism does not imply the stronger, but the stronger does imply the weaker. This defence of liberalism assumes that the stronger form of scepticism has not been established beyond doubt, a contention which will be argued for in chapter 5.

We can now summarize how a liberal position, formulated in terms of the rights of individuals, can be justified by this unconventional form of consequentialist reasoning. Such rights are not to be seen as conditions for the existence of this or that particular activity. For respect for those rights, in certain circumstances, can be disadvantageous from the point of view of someone who is already committed to the view that what is valuable lies in some other particular activity. Nevertheless, the idea that rights are conditions for something, as distinct from maximizing something, can be put to use. The liberal rights are conditions for having more reasonable views about what activities are worth while: they are conditions for people choosing between activities which already exist, or, more rarely, for attempting to create new ones. It is not suggested, of course, that it is inevitable that if people are free to choose, they will always make good choices; nor that if their freedom to choose is restricted, they will never engage in worthwhile activities.

Why should we suppose that if people's freedom to choose between various activities is protected by certain rights, people may come to have more reasonable views about which activities are worth while? The only way in which this could be shown is, apparently, to take examples of societies in which these rights are generally respected and to contrast what happens with those in which they are not. One would hope to show that when the rights are generally respected more progress is made in discerning what is good than when they are not. One might recall Mill's contrast between the stagnation of 'closed' Chinese civilisation and the progress of 'open' Western European civilisation.[3] But such an argument presupposes that we at least partially know what it is more or less reasonable to believe is good, and we may not wish to take such an exposed stand in order to defend the claim. We do not have Mill's confidence in identifying when progress has occurred.

However, there is another kind of argument available which does not rely on such contentious assumptions. Consider any state of affairs about which you accept that it is possible to have more or less reasonable beliefs. What we believe is partly influenced by the evidence those situations provide for the truth or falsity of certain beliefs. But it is also influenced by our interest in believing certain things to be true or false about those situations. For example, it may be that if we were to believe that P is true of situation S, most people would think our belief ridiculous, and we have an interest in not appearing ridiculous. The chances of believing what is true must be greater the less our beliefs are influenced by considerations of interest and the more they are influenced by the evidence. On some matters, such as whether the door is open, we are nearly always wholly influenced by the evidence. On other matters, where important interests are at stake, those interests well may affect our beliefs more than the evidence. If you have been brought up in the Catholic Church (or the Communist Party), with most of your associates Catholics (or Communists), there will be powerful considerations of interest inclining you towards the acceptance of the central tenets of Catholicism (or Communism) quite apart from the evidence. That is not to say, of course, that one will always have reasonable beliefs on matters where one's interests are not involved, and fail to have them when one's interests are involved.

If it is allowed that certain activities could be of 'objective' value, we may similarly distinguish between the evidence for the presence of such value, and our interest in supposing that they are, or are not, of value. (Non-cognitivists would have difficulty in making such a distinction. I am presupposing, but shall not argue here for, the falsity of non-cognitivism.) My case for certain rights of individuals is that they eliminate one kind of powerful consideration of

interest for believing things to be of value quite apart from
the evidence. This is not to say, of course, that respect for
such rights eliminates all heteronomous influences of interest
on what we believe.

There are additional considerations favouring rights of
self-ownership. Unless a person has the right to control his
or her own body and mind, there will not be adequate
protection of the choices of each person, which is necessary
in order that there should be as many independent views as
possible on what is worth while in itself. If you have no right
to your own opinion, but are forced to parrot someone
else's, your opinion makes no contribution to the discovery
of what it is reasonable to believe. Rights of self-ownership
also are to be preferred to an arrangement in which every
person has an equal share in the ownership of all persons.
With rights of self-ownership each individual can take the
initiative in exploring what is worth while in itself, whereas
with equal joint ownership it is only the collective that can
take the initiative.[4] Furthermore, there should be equal
rights of self-ownership because a system which denied such
rights to some could not be expected to be as effective in
reaching more reasonable views about what is worthwhile in
itself. The views of some would be arbitrarily excluded.

So far nothing has been said about a favourite liberal
notion – self-realization, and the exposition of my conception of liberalism may appropriately conclude with some
remarks on that idea. The conception of liberalism presented
here implies that the goal of self-realization is acceptable,
but that it has a dependent status. We may contrast two
conceptions of self-realization. The first simply signifies the
idea that a person's potentialities, whatever they might be,
are given their full, appropriate expression. No judgement is
made of the desirability of what is realized. In this sense
Stalin achieved self-realization: the appropriate expression
of a vicious and hideously deformed personality. The second
implies that the potentialities brought to their realization are
good. It is in the latter sense that liberals endorse the goal of
self-realization. Thus when they write of a person having

realized certain potentialities, it is assumed that what has been realized is good. As the term is standardly used by liberals, the lives of Mozart and Tolstoy would be cases of persons having realized themselves, but not the lives of Hitler and Stalin.

As judgements about self-realization presuppose views about what it is good or desirable for persons to become, they depend on our having reasonable views about what is good or worth while. If we are to say that a person has made progress towards her self-realization in a certain direction, such as musical composition, we assume that there is an established human activity, with its internal standards for what counts as better or worse performance, and that she has performed creditably by reference to those standards. But we also endorse this activity as good and worth while. Methods of torture have a long tradition, and no doubt some practitioners have considerable sophistication, but we do not think that a good torturer is one variety of the self-realized personality.

It is not suggested, of course, that these conceptions of what is worth while are agreed upon by everyone. Some may regard a monastic life as a possible form of self-realization, others not, as they do not see anything of value in such a life. It is also true that exceptionally gifted practitioners of certain human activities sometimes effect changes in the accepted standards of those activities, or, in very rare cases, create new activities.

Is knowledge of what is good good?

We must now consider some apparent objections to this position (apart from the assumptions made about our knowledge of what is of intrinsic value, which will be considered in chapter 5). The first objection points out that this defence of liberalism is said not to depend on any claim to know that this or that is good. But it is said that certain rights may be defended on the ground that they are conditions for coming to have more reasonable beliefs about what is good. Is this not to presuppose that the attempt to acquire knowledge of what is good is itself good: in effect, to elevate the search for what is intrinsically good into what is intrinsically good? It appears that this defence of liberalism rests on a claim to know what is good after all.

To answer this it is necessary to clarify the reasons for thinking that it is good to attempt to acquire more reasonable beliefs about what is good. On what grounds would it be reasonable to deny that the attempt to gain knowledge of what is good is good? If we already know that something is good, and that it is not possible that anything else should be good, then the attempt to acquire knowledge of what is good is redundant. Such a position is taken by classical utilitarians, and it will later be suggested that it is implausible. If we know that we cannot have knowledge of what is good, then the attempt to acquire such knowledge is senseless. This is the position I have called 'strong scepticism' and which later will be shown to be implausible. But if it is possible to gain knowledge of what is good, although we do not as yet have such knowledge, then it is evident that it is good to attempt to acquire knowledge of what is good. This holds even for the person who professes to be uninterested in the goodness of anything unless he can have it for himself. For even if one's interest in the good is self-preoccupied, one still has reason to be concerned that what one tries to get for oneself is good. Egotism can be thwarted not only when another rather than oneself gets what is good, but also when one gets what one wants and it proves not to be good.

If this argument is correct, there is reason for thinking that the attempt to acquire knowledge of what is good is itself good. But this does not require a commitment to the view that the attempt to acquire such knowledge is intrinsically good. Some, of course, would maintain that such an attempt is itself intrinsically good. I am unsure whether this is so. In any case it is not essential to this defence of liberalism to claim that the attempt to acquire knowledge of what is good is itself intrinsically good.

Certainly the view that we know that the attempt to acquire knowledge of what is intrinsically good is itself intrinsically good must be avoided if we are to remain consistent.

From anyone's point of view it is good to have more reasonable views about what is good in itself. One basis on which some might wish to advance this position is the claim that any addition to knowledge is intrinsically good, and therefore that additional knowledge of what is intrinsically good is good. This is not the basis being used here. For it is open to doubt whether knowledge is intrinsically good. The goodness of some increment to knowledge would appear to depend on context. And if knowledge is not intrinsically good, it is open to question whether it is always good in other ways. The reason why having more reasonable views of what is intrinsically good is good from anyone's point of view is that we would not wish to pursue illusory conceptions of what is intrinsically good.

May we explore all conceptions of what is good?

Does my approach to defending liberalism entirely take seriously the idea that people should be at liberty to explore any conception of what is good? Is it not in fact assumed that any conception of the good people will be free to explore will be one consistent with respect for certain rights it is assumed everyone has, such as a right to life? This would seem to imply that certain conceptions of what is good are to be ruled out in advance – for example, those that see the most admirable life as one displaying the military virtues, or as lying in some kind of life of violence. It may be added that these are not highly eccentric conceptions of what is valuable, adopted by only a few queer people. They are conceptions of the good upon which whole cultures have been founded, and which are still to be found in some sub-cultures today.

(It is not suggested that I, personally, believe that there is anything of intrinsic value to be found in situations of violent conflict. The apparently quite common contrary belief is probably due to the intense experiences provoked by such situations. But while the perception of that which is believed to be of intrinsic value is often an intense experience, not all intense experiences are caused by the presence of something of intrinsic value. In this case it is more likely that intense experiences are caused by powerful natural instincts being called into play.)

Is the liberal seriously suggesting, then, that anyone should be at liberty to follow these conceptions of what is worth while? If not, must there not be some reason why pursuit of these conceptions of what is good is to be ruled out? Is this form of liberalism making the arbitrary assumption that what is good·or worth while does not lie in certain directions?[5]

An answer to this problem which bluntly claims that any liberal society must rest on some agreement or tacit understanding that certain conceptions of what is worth while will not be explored is to be avoided. For this would represent liberal societies as well as non-liberal ones as based on broad agreement about what forms of life are worth while, and the difference from non-liberal societies would be at most one of degree. There is a less impromptu line of reply. Those who have become committed to a certain form of life, and with that to a particular view of what is good, have a natural interest, i.e. a self-regarding interest, in others following that form of life also. One reason for such an interest is that it is not possible to pursue a view of what is a worthwhile activity except in a social context, i.e. in the company of those who have a similar view of what is good. No one could be an opera singer or a philosopher alone, in the sense of being quite detached from a tradition in which these activities are pursued. Therefore anyone has an interest in there not being too few people involved in one's chosen activities. In addition, the more who are involved in that activity the more probable it is that some who follow it will have outstanding talent at it, making its pursuit more rewarding.

A further point is that people who follow a certain activity may find that the pursuit by others of different activities has a tendency to undermine· their confidence in the pursuit of their own activity. An example was the tendency of some circles in the nineteenth century to see the pursuit of scientific research as undermining the confidence of the religious. (It is not to the point of this argument to decide whether it is reasonable for followers of one form of life to find the following of another inimical to their ends: it is only assumed that they do in fact believe this. There are other cases, of course, where we do not think that there is any conflict between the pursuit of one conception of what is worth while and another.) In cases where there is believed to be conflict those of one group may see themselves as having an interest in not being unsettled in their convictions by those who pursue the 'conflicting' activity. Therefore they may see themselves as having an interest in silencing, or in some way restricting, the activities of those in the other group.

If liberalism is justified as the set of preconditions necessary for the attempt to discover what is good, it will not serve this purpose if people pursue some form of activity, not out of any conviction that something of worth may be contained in it, but merely to avoid threats of harm and disadvantage to themselves. If that is the reason a person follows a certain activity, the commitment is based on a 'heteronomous' motive. Thus there is a case, from the point of view of the present theory, for restricting the grosser forms of coercion which can be used to make people follow certain forms of activity rather than others.

But the objection may be pressed further. The equal assignment of rights of self-ownership imposes a fixed framework within which persons may choose what they consider to be worth while modes of existence. Those choices are restricted by the framework. Now my position is not that these rights are, in some Lockean sense, self-evident and can be established without reference to any conception of what is good. Nor is it my position that they are to be established by reference to a specific view of what is good, as in the case of regular forms of consequentialism. If my conception of liberalism takes an experimental attitude towards what modes of existence are worth while, how can this be consistent with restricting those choices in the way rights of self-ownership do?

My reply is that respect for rights of self-ownership at most places restrictions on the manner in which a conception of what is worth while may be pursued: it does not exclude any conception of what is worth while. Take again the case of those who see as worth while the military virtues and certain forms of violence. The liberal objection to this is that such people often wish to practise their view of what is worth while on the unwilling. And as the participation of these people is unwilling, the point of pursuing this activity is defeated from the liberal point of view. It is true that if there really were instances of people wishing to engage in such activities with others of a like mind, in a way that did not injure anyone but the willing participants, there should be no objection on my view. And there may be instances to be found in some violent subcultures – for example, boxing. There still remains an inconsistency between this view and the view of existing legal systems, which prohibit private violence even with consent, except for very few cases, such as some sports. Perhaps the existing legal view can be justified on the basis of one or other (or both) of the following considerations. (1) It is very difficult, in practice, to ensure that non-consenting persons do not get harmed in some way. (2) It is very difficult to establish that participation was not coerced.

The suggestion that respect for rights of self-ownership implies no advance restriction on what modes of existence may be chosen may still meet with disbelief. For one thing, it is obvious that some modes of existence can be described which would be ruled out by respect for rights of self-ownership – for example, leading the life of a bandit, rapist, or member of the Mafia – and some might regard such lives in a favourable light. Or what of a certain kind of Fascist attitude which celebrates the will to power and domination? What is thought to be good here is precisely the destruction or domination of the unwilling; of those who do not consent to be treated in these ways. And something similar may be present in the motives of the rapist or the mobster. To insist that all pursuit of what is worth while should be founded on consent is necessarily to exclude this conception of what is worth while. Few are likely to sympathize with this conception, but that, it may be said, is not to the point: it is a conception which, regrettably, has had many adherents, in Nazi Germany in the past, and apparently amongst some contemporary white South Africans. It is true, no doubt, that this view is not consistent with recognizing the equality of man: it must be assumed that there is some 'lesser' kind of person whom it is proper to treat in this way if one can. But I cannot consistently appeal to whatever good grounds there may be for such equality, for my case is that the equal assignment of rights of self-ownership is justified on the basis that such an assignment is necessary for better-formed views about what is worth while in itself. The counter-argument is that this assignment simply excludes certain views.

We could dispose of this counter-argument if we could be sure that no such conception of what is worth while is correct. One argument, which derives from the concept of intrinsic value, and anticipates a later discussion, starts with the assertion that if something is of intrinsic value then *it* is that which is of value (i.e. the value is solely dependent on what *it* is like). Therefore something cannot be of intrinsic value because you desire it, for that would be to make the value it has entirely dependent on something external to it: your desiring it. Now a member of the 'superior' group no doubt could desire to dominate, but a member of the 'inferior' group would not desire to be dominated. Therefore the desirability of this domination is wholly dependent on the desires of the 'superior' group, and so it could not be of intrinsic value.

This argument is unsuccessful. It is true that if a member

of the 'superior' group desires to dominate solely because he has the desire to do so, then he does not regard his dominating as of intrinsic value. But this need not be the correct characterization of his desire to dominate. His considering it desirable that he should dominate may make no particular reference to his desires. He may desire to dominate as a 'superior' kind of person, and nothing has been said that would rule out that as desirable in itself. Even if it is 'psychologically' impossible that a member of the 'inferior' group should desire that he should be dominated, it is nevertheless possible that his being dominated should be desirable.

We might compare the present case with another example, that where both of two enemies, A and B, consider it desirable in itself to be a conqueror. A desires that A conquers, i.e. that A has that which is desirable, and similarly for B. That A desires this desirable thing for himself, and desires that B should not have it, does not imply that he cannot think that what B has, if B conquers A, is desirable in itself. Thus even if it is true that members of the 'inferior' group cannot ('psychologically') desire that they should be subject to the will of the 'superior' group, it is still possible, so far as the concept of intrinsic value is concerned, that it is desirable in itself that the 'superior' group should dominate. Someone in the 'inferior' group might also consider domination desirable, though not, presumably, that he should be a dominated one.

It must be confessed, therefore, that there is no way, from the point of view of my conception of liberalism, of permitting people to follow ideas of what is worth while which necessarily exclude the consent of some participating in those activities. It is some comfort that from the point of view of another argument for rights of self-ownership – the conditions for a stable *modus vivendi* with minimal coercion – the pursuit of such conceptions of what is worth while must be excluded. So there was no serious possibility of an acceptable political order accepting the pursuit of such conceptions of what is worth while. Nevertheless it would have have been agreeable to have found an argument to show that such conceptions of what is worth while must be mistaken.

'Command' liberalism

In chapter 1 it was suggested that liberalism should be characterized in terms of a set of rights of self-ownership. A justification has now been proposed for why such rights should be assigned to all persons, from the point of view of attaining more reasonable views about which activities are of value. It is desirable that there should be as many independent views as possible on what activities are of value. If not all persons were assigned rights of self-ownership, and some therefore could be under a non-contractual obligation to engage in such activities as others might choose to direct, then the fact that they were engaging in certain activities would be no indication of their choice or judgement concerning the worth of such activities. Alternatively, if we were to suppose, not that some were subject to the control of others, but that each was subject to the control of all (as would be the case if there were equal joint ownership of all persons by all persons, deciding collectively), the independent choice and judgement of each would be confined to his or her contribution to the collective choice process.

There is an objection to this argument. If a person is to engage in virtually any activity, the co-operation of some others will be necessary. If all enjoy rights of self-ownership, then any one individual may be unable to engage in an activity of his or her choice because of the lack of willing co-operation on the part of others, i.e. because no one else chooses to exercise his or her rights of self-ownership in an appropriate way. Would it not be justifiable on my view for the rights of self-ownership of some to be compromised to some extent if this is necessary for others to engage in activities that otherwise would not be open to them?

It is worth noting, to begin with, that in practice the barriers faced by the unorthodox have not been of this character. For example, the difficulties encountered in living the life of a homosexual in the past would not usually have been the absence of other homosexuals, but a refusal on the part of the law or the majority of the society to accept fully the implications of the rights of self-ownership. Most human activities thought to have been of value do not require very many other willing participants, so there is a good chance that others can be found, at least if another implication of rights of self-ownership, freedom of movement, is accepted; and the unconventional are able to gather together. Nevertheless it is possible, even if in practice unlikely, that the consideration mentioned would be an obstacle to some engaging in activities of their choice. Even in these circumstances, however, it would be undesirable to make co-operation mandatory (i.e. to compromise the rights of self-ownership of others) because unwilling participation in an activity will not contribute to more reasonable views about what is of value. A person's engaging in an activity is, as such, no evidence of its value: it is only if that person is engaging in it because of being attracted to it that participation evinces a belief in its value for its own sake.

The importance of conviction in the exploration of what is worth while is one reason for avoiding what might be called a 'command' liberal state. Certain possibilities for what is worth while are apt to be followed by many, others neglected. Why not compromise the rights of some individuals and direct them to explore neglected possibilities?[6] The search for what is worth while in itself is not a co-operative enterprise in the way that exploring an unknown tract of land can be, each person being assigned his particular area to explore. In order for exploration of what is of value in itself to have any point, it must be motivated by conviction and inclination.

The importance of motivation makes it reasonable that no one should have the right to coerce others into joining with him in the pursuit of a certain activity. However, coercion is not the only possibility. People are attracted to engaging in certain activities not only (and not usually) because of the conviction that these activities are of value in themselves, but because they foresee possible gains in terms of wealth, status, and so on. Suppose, then, that there are certain activities which do not 'get off the ground' because too few people are interested in pursuing them. Why should not means be made available to encourage people to pursue these activities, at least to the point where they become viable and self-sustaining? It could be objected that nothing worth while can be expected to emerge if people engage in activities for 'heteronomous' reasons. But it is not clear why this must be so, and in any case, why should not people do something worth while, even if personal advantage is a major motivation? And motives may be mixed: a person may believe that following a certain activity is worth while in itself, but not be inclined to follow it because the disadvantages in other ways are too great, or the advantages in other ways are too few. It would seem that liberalism of the form proposed here is committed to the view that, other things being equal, the variety of distinct and possibly good forms of activity should be as great as possible. It is difficult to see what objection there could be to encouraging minority, and not otherwise viable, forms of activity if it is desirable, as liberals are apt to suppose, that an education system should be, in part, a process of acquainting a new generation with the existing variety of activities believed to contain elements of what is good, this process being sustained, at least in part, from the community's resources.

It must be allowed that the assignment of rights of self-ownership will not always create the situation a liberal finds most desirable. Some may choose to exercise their rights of self-ownership by way of slavishly following the lead of others. It is also possible that most people may be of a conservative temper, viewing new 'modes of existence' with suspicion, and providing little encouragement to the unconventional. A further possibility is that some will choose to exercise their rights of self-ownership in such a way that the unconventional are ostracized. If people have rights of self-ownership it follows that they have the right to choose with whom they will or will not associate. They may, therefore, choose not to associate with those who are unconventional out of disapproval of the unconventional, and this may be a considerable disincentive to being unconventional. But these possibilities are not reasons for going back on an assignment of rights of self-ownership. For it is extremely doubtful whether any alternative assignment of rights (for example, one which gave the conventional limited rights to disapprove) would be better overall. Some group of persons would have to be given the right to decide what counted as 'unwarranted disapproval', and this would be likely to be a much greater threat to liberty than disapproval of the unconventional by the conventional. The appropriate remedy is the cultivation of a liberal virtue – a tolerant temper – alongside respect for everyone's rights of. self-ownership.

Paternalism

We have defended the right of individuals not to be coerced into engaging in activities others may consider to be worth while. May a person be prevented from engaging in any activity because it would be harmful to him? Is 'paternalism' permissible?

Implacable opposition to paternalism is thought by some to be an indispensable aspect of any position which could be called 'liberal'. On the conception of liberalism defended here not all forms of paternalism are unacceptable. There are two ways in which an activity may be regarded as harmful. It may be harmful to a person's physical well-being: there may be a risk of dying prematurely, incurring some physical incapacity, or becoming prone to certain kinds of illness. We know beyond reasonable doubt that the consequences of some activities are harmful in this sense. Alternatively, the consequences of an activity may be said to be harmful in that they worsen a person's moral character, intellectual development, or proper sense of the relative importance of things. In this sense too we can claim to know what is or is not harmful, but this will be relative to a certain view of how a person should be: diligent, creative, or intellectually rigorous. We cannot claim to know that the supposed good by reference to which these judgements are made really is good.

Paternalistic attempts to avoid harm of the latter kind – 'moral harm', as it might be termed – are not permissible in the case of normal adults. No one is in a position to establish that the supposed harm really is such, except relative to some presumed conception of what is good. It may be true that if a person fails to cultivate certain traits of character he will fail to 'get on' in certain social circles, but to regard this as harm assumes that what the circle regards as worth while really is so. Suppose conscription existed, not because of concern about national security, but because the establishment held that the experience of military discipline cultivated fine moral characters in young people. This would be an impermissible form of paternalism because it presupposes a particular (and to my mind, absurd) view of how people should be.

To this general claim about 'moral' harm an exception must be allowed. Respect for rights of self-ownership is not an 'optional' moral requirement from a liberal point of view, by contrast with, say, diligence. It is therefore permissible that attempts should be made to encourage the liberal virtues of respect for the rights of self-ownership of others and tolerance, and in so far as people are deflected from these virtues they are harmed.

Now let us turn to interference for the sake of a person's physical welfare: to such requirements as compulsory chest X-rays, vaccinations, wearing of seat-belts and hard hats, and the carrying of life-jackets on private pleasure-craft. In such cases it can be established beyond reasonable doubt that these requirements are desirable for a person's physical welfare. Now whatever may be a person's conception of what is worth while for its own sake, prima facie he will desire his own physical welfare. And as, in normal cases, these paternalistic requirements are neutral with respect to a person's conception of what is worth while, and do not rule out engaging in any significant conception of what is worth while, there would seem to be no objection to them from a liberal point of view. To make the compulsory wearing of seat-belts a great issue of personal liberty is a mockery of the liberal tradition. While such paternalistic measures do not derive from the present conception of liberalism, neither are they incompatible with it.

But it may be objected that there are cases in which to insist on paternalistic measures of this kind would be in direct conflict with some people's conception of what is worth while. There are physically dangerous activities such as boxing, mountain climbing, and motor racing. There is the very common case of people working too hard at something they find enjoyable and worth while for the good of their health. Prohibiting such activities out of concern for physical well-being is scarcely compatible with neutrality about what is worth while in itself. It is one thing to say that everyone is prima facie concerned for his own physical well-being, and another to insist that that concern should outweigh any other consideration with which it may come into conflict. It would appear, then, that where paternalism (in order to prevent harm of the first kind) would impinge significantly on a person's conception of what is worth while it should not be allowed. It may seem strange to insist that a driver should wear a seat-belt while not preventing a dangerous mountaineering expedition, when the danger involved in the latter is so much greater. But the first prohibition does not affect anyone's conception of what is worth while, while the second would.

Is this sketch of a liberal position on paternalism consistent with the view that persons have rights of self-ownership? Two doubts may be expressed. It would seem that if one accepts rights of self-ownership, one must accept a right of suicide. But if it is permissible for people to take their own lives, why should they be expected to conform to minor paternalistic restrictions? The answer is that conformity to minor paternalistic requirements makes no difference to a person's pursuit of what is worth while, whereas the insistence that a person should continue to live may be very important in the light of that person's conception of what is worth while. To continue to live in certain circumstances (for example, in what is regarded as disgrace) may be intolerable from the point of view of a certain person's conception of what is worth while. (We are here considering, of course, the judgements of mature adults.)

There is a second ground for doubting consistency. If persons have rights of self-ownership, surely that excludes interference with a person for his own good, just as private-property rights exclude your interfering when I let my house go to rack and ruin (provided my neglect is not affecting anyone else's property)? It is not clear that this is so. To say that persons have rights of self-ownership does not imply that a person may control that over which he has such rights in any way he chooses. Your arm is yours, something over which you have rights, but that does not imply that you may use it to bar my way. But this, it will be said, is not to the point. Your barring my way is a violation of my right to pass, but a person's neglect of his own well-being is not a violation of anyone else's (anyway, non-contractual) rights.

An interpretation of rights of self-ownership must be provided on the basis of what is seen as the justification for those rights. To revert to the example of private-property rights, not all conceptions of such rights would confer on an owner a right to the gross neglect of his property. Similarly the interpretation we give to rights of self-ownership will be related to the justification for such rights. If the process of attaining more reasonable views of what is worth while would not be affected by some forms of paternalistic interference, it can be allowed that rights of self-ownership do not preclude such interference.

There is another circumstance, however, in which the ground for justifying rights of self-ownership would appear to require the suspension of those rights in a more serious way than we have yet considered. To the contention that attempts to acquire knowledge of what is good are good, let us add that, so far as we know, only human beings have the potential to acquire knowledge of what is good. It follows that it is good that human beings should continue to exist. Now under the present conception of liberalism everyone has the right to engage, or not to engage, in any activity he or she considers to be worth while, so long as this does not violate anyone else's rights. This includes the right to choose whether to engage in procreative activity, because the choice to do so (with consenting partners) or not does not violate anyone else's rights.[7] Now suppose no one were to choose to engage in such activity. This is undesirable if it is good to attempt to acquire knowledge of what is good, and the continued existence of people is necessary for this. But by the present conception of liberalism no one has the right to require anyone to engage in such activity. If no one will procreate unless the principle is violated, should the rights of some then be violated? As the defence of the original conception is consequentialist, there appears to be no alternative to saying that rights may be violated in such an (admittedly highly unlikely) situation.

Equality

It has been claimed that the form of liberalism defended here implies an equal assignment of rights of self-ownership to all 'normal' adults. In terms of the view being advanced here, this amounts to the claim that all ought to be regarded as equal in the sense that all have an equal right to express and act on their view of what is good. But is this claim plausible? Might it not be that some people are more likely to make a correct choice as to which activities are worth while than others? Does this position not imply a certain form of elitism: an elite of those who are especially well qualified to discern what is good?

Some are likely to make a better choice than others, in that some have been acquainted with a wider variety of activities generally thought to be good. Again, some, because of their practical circumstances, have a stronger vested interest in believing certain activities to contain elements of what is good, and may allow themselves to be deceived by these interests. So it is plausible that those who enjoy the benefits of a good education (in the liberal sense) and who have the good fortune to be relieved of pressing practical concerns, will be better placed to discern what is good. But these differences between people are due to the contingencies of their particular situations, and do not justify us in believing that there are (or would be, if such factors did not operate) differences between people in their potential as choosers of what is good. It should be added that if it could be established that there were 'innate' differences between people in intelligence this would not settle the matter, for it is far from clear that as a chooser of what is good intelligence is the only, or the most important, factor.

It might be thought that the assignment of rights ought to be biased towards those who are 'more perceptive'. To claim that one person is more perceptive of value than another is to presuppose that we have some knowledge of where values lies. For we say that someone is imperceptive if he fails to see value in that which we believe to be of value, of if he sees value in that which we believe to have none. Now it is true that such judgements of perceptiveness and imperceptiveness acquire a certain 'objectivity' in that there may be a consensus in a particular cultural tradition at a particular time that certain things are of value. So by reference to such a consensus we can claim 'objectively' that a person is perceptive or otherwise. But to assign differential rights on the basis of differences in perceptiveness established in this way would be to take as final those judgements of value that happen to be made at a particular stage of a cultural tradition. To some extent such judgements may have to be made use of in a liberal society (as will be suggested in chapter 4), but it would not be acceptable to use them in making a basic assignment of rights. Too often art forms, for example, which have been thought 'crude', 'vulgar', 'common', or 'primitive' by the 'perceptive' of a particular period have come to be acknowledged by the 'perceptive' of a later period as of value (for example, jazz and impressionism).

But perhaps there is better reason for an unequal assignment of rights. Some people are energetic in the pursuit of their goals and willing to explore many possibilities. Do not these people deserve better rights than the lethargic? In this case there would appear to be no appeal to assumed knowledge of value: we do not ask which goals are being more energetically pursued, but simply point out that the energetic are making a greater contribution to the search for what is of value.[8]

This ground for an unequal assignment of rights also rests on an assumption about what we know to be of value, but this is less obvious than in the previous case. It is apt to be assumed in the Western tradition that what is of value will be discovered only through energetic activity. This is closely related to the idea that that which is of value will be some kind of human construction; and a tendency to suppose, other things being equal, that the more elaborate that construction, the more likely it will be of value. But this is the view of only one tradition, even if deeply embedded in that tradition. There is also the view that the discernment of what is of value requires calm, contemplation, and a certain passivity – a detachment from one's own particular practical ends. Anxious concern about getting to one's destination on time makes it unlikely one will appreciate the beauty of the landscape. To assign superior rights to the more energetic would be to assume that the former tradition is correct.

Consideration has been given to arguments against an equal assignment of rights of self-ownership. But even an equal assignment of such rights may be objected to by some egalitarians. They may point out that if everyone has equal rights of self-ownership, and everything that arises from a legitimate exercise of such rights is legitimate, then such an assignment of rights may legitimise inequality.

It is true, as egalitarians claim, that the equal assignment of such rights can give rise to legitimate inequality.[9] Consider the case of Immanuel, an eminent philosopher. An aspect of Immanuel's rights of control over his person is his right to express philosophical views to others willing to listen. Other philosophers have similar rights of control, including the right to choose whether to pay attention to what another philosopher says. Immanuel exercises his rights of control and expresses his thoughts: other philosophers exercise their rights of control and attend to Immanuel's ideas. Many choose to take notice of Immanuel's thoughts, and few choose to take notice of the ideas of other philosophers. Certain inequalities between philosophers arise, one of which could be described as an inequality of power: people are much more influenced by what Immanuel thinks than by what other philosophers think. Immanuel's exercise of his rights may also reduce certain freedoms of others. Another philosopher may want to discuss his own views, but find no other philosopher with whom he is free to do so, because the others have chosen to spend their time attending to Immanuel. Had it not been for the interest aroused by Immanuel's views this philosopher might have found himself free to discuss his own ideas with some of the others. This absence of a freedom of a certain kind is, of course, compatible with the presence of freedoms of other kinds: for example, freedom from an authority preventing this philosopher from discussing his views with anyone else.

In order to distinguish sharply between inequality arising from the exercise of rights of self-ownership and inequality arising from the exercise of private-property rights (which will be considered in chapter 4), we can suppose that our philosophers live in an egalitarian socialist society. There is a national income norm, and Immanuel can make no more money from his eminence than any other person. Nor are there any publicly recognized gradations of formal status. Routine economic tasks are shared by everyone, activities such as philosophy being carried on in the time left over which, let us suppose, is considerable. Though the inequality between Immanuel's reputation and that of other philosophers has none of the consequential economic and social inequalities it would have in an existing society, in equalities arising wholly out of the exercise of people's rights of self-ownership are nevertheless important to them.

Inequalities arising from exercises of rights of self-ownership cannot be wholly insulated from economic inequalities. Suppose that in this egalitarian socialist society Immanuel offers instruction in philosophy not in exchange for money, but for services of others which Immanuel values (such as having his hair cut). It is difficult to see how such an exchange could be objected to by anyone who accepts rights of self-ownership, at least so long as the exchange concerns services which are wholly people's actions.[10] If Immanuel's instruction is very popular he might become, in terms of the contractual obligations he has accumulated, quite 'wealthy', and it is difficult to see how such inequalities of 'wealth' could be objected to by anyone who accepts rights of self-ownership. I am supposing, but shall not here argue for, the view that to allow this much in the way of 'free market transactions' will not be the undoing of the egalitarian socialist society. To avoid inconsistency with the earlier assumptions we may suppose that Immanuel may not avoid his contribution to routine economic tasks through such transactions, and that he may not exchange his services for 'goods' or 'means of production'.

It is a further consequence of accepting rights of self-ownership that an arrangement legitimately entered into by two or more persons may adversely affect third parties. Suppose some philosophers have remained aloof from fashion. Immanuel's reputation has not arisen through their exercise of rights of control. (It has arisen despite it.) Yet members of the minority may have their position worsened as compared with what it would have been had Immanuel and his admirers exercised their rights differently. One of the minority might have been the most eminent philosopher

had it not been for Immanuel and his admirers. If we believe
that people have rights of self-ownership, the worsening of
the position of third parties is beside the point in determining the rightfulness of the situation so long as rights are
not violated. Of course we may take a low view of the moral
character of someone who is oblivious of, or indifferent to,
the effects on others of legitimate exercises of rights of self-
ownership.

It may be that if the separation between rewards from
exercises of rights of self-ownership and economic rewards
is kept as strict as in this example there would be few
egalitarians who would object to the inequalities that could
arise. Certainly it would seem that egalitarians principally
have in mind the consequent economic and status advantages
the talented may receive in a capitalist society. I have yet to
learn of an egalitarian who begrudged Kant, Mozart and
Tolstoy their fame.

Community

It might be thought that the position defended here
denigrates co-operative human activity and community. It is
true that my defence of liberalism upholds certain rights of
individuals. But this does not imply that co-operative
activity is unimportant in the pursuit of what is worth while
in itself. Those activities believed to be worth while in
themselves will be pursued in association with others.
Progress in understanding what is worth while in itself
hardly could be due entirely to one individual. New work,
even when the work of only one person, is always presented
to an 'audience' (in some sense). Whether that work is
accepted as valuable will depend on the response, over time,
of those to whom it is presented. All the creations we
believe to be worth while are, at least in this sense, co-
operative. A further sense in which they are co-operative is
that they are always located in a tradition of, for example,
artistic, intellectual, or religious forms.

John Gray contrasts Mill's view of 'experiments in living', which are 'affairs of the individual in which he asserts his inborn individuality against the pressures of social convention' with Hayek's, in which they are undertaken 'by distinct traditions or ways of life which compete for practitioners'.[11] It is scarcely necessary to enter such a debate from the point of view of my defence of liberalism. For on both Mill's and Hayek's view it is necessary that persons should have rights of self-ownership: in the case of Hayek's position, so that they can migrate from one tradition to another. Members of a tradition cannot have the right to overrule the rights of self-ownership of their members, for that would make migration impossible. So whichever view is taken of how 'experiments in living' proceed, rights of self-ownership are desirable.

It is not a consequence of the position presented here that individuals should constantly question what they hold to be of worth, rather than actually pursuing their own beliefs about what is of value. A particular view of what is of value cannot be effectively explored unless it is pursued with conviction and enthusiasm. It is true that if everyone has the right to pursue 'modes of existence' he or she considers worth while, then those some pursue will seem 'opposed' to those of others, and this can erode some people's confidence. But this is not so serious an obstacle to the pursuit of a given view of what is worth while as to make it impossible for most people. As people nearly always pursue such views in the company of the like-minded, they are not usually affected very much by those who have 'opposed' views. In any case, forbidding the exploration of certain 'modes of existence' would provide only a false sense of security for those who pursued the remainder: the only real sense of security comes from knowing that others have had the opportunity to question, and have failed to shake one's confidence.

Those who wish to press the claims of community may advance a further, more subtle, argument against my position. Liberals claim that their position is neutral as between competing conceptions of what is worth while in itself. But it might be said that an assignment of rights of self-ownership is in fact biased towards certain conceptions of what is worth while and against others. Some conceptions of what is worth while are underpinned by respect for obligations which are thought of as having non-voluntary grounds. Religious devotion in the Christian tradition has been thought of in this way. For example: from the point of view of a believer one does not choose to have an obligation to worship God. Or to take a secular example, most people's conception of the worth of family life involves the idea that obligations to children and parents are non-voluntary. Will not the assignment of rights of self-ownership discriminate against such conceptions of what is worth while in favour of others more obviously related to individual choice, such as romantic love? (It might be thought definitive of certain kinds of relationship, and what is valuable about them, that they depend only on the choice of each party, and that if either were to consider that he or she had an obligation towards the other it would be a different kind of relationship and, if valuable, valuable in a different way.) Possibly those conceptions of what is worth while favoured by the assignment of rights of self-ownership have less to recommend them than those that are not. But certainly, some are favoured, and others are not; contrary to liberal protestations.

Rights of self-ownership may be defended on the ground that they are desirable in order to have more reasonable views about what is worth while without it being implied that activities depending on the possession of such rights are the most worth while. Even those who are convinced that all worth while activities are based on non-voluntary obligations have reason to favour the assignment of rights of self-ownership. For there are conflicting views about what is worth while amongst those who hold that all worth while activities are based on non-voluntary obligations. For example, some will hold that one has a non-voluntary obligation to seek salvation in one way, others in another. It would seem that there is no way of knowing which is correct other than through processes involving the assignment of rights of self-ownership.

But is it not paradoxical to say that people must be free to choose which, if any, non-voluntary obligation they accept? Not if we distinguish the viewpoint of the individual from the viewpoint of the neutral framework of the liberal state. An individual within that framework may take an obligation to be non-revisable and independent of his choice, while from the point of view of the framework the acceptance of that obligation is a matter of individual choice and not imposed by the framework. It is true that a person who accepts such an obligation as independent of his choice could hardly be unaware that others regard it differently; and that the situation is not the same as that in which, in a non-liberal political order, everyone takes it for granted that it is not a matter of individual choice. (An example would be the obligation to worship God as seen throughout most of Christian history.) But it still could be that in a liberal society most activities chosen were ones in which the participants regarded themselves as having non-revisable obligations. So those who, in this sense, place value on community have nothing to fear from the present form of liberalism. If they still insist that, in this conception of the liberal society, no one could adopt non-optional obligations with the same innocence as has been possible in the past, that is true: but that innocence is irrecoverable, not because of my version of liberalism, but because of history.

It may be thought that there is an argument for community in a stronger sense than this. It may be pointed out that what a person *is*, in most significant respects, is the result of the community in which he lives – its language, customs, culture, and so on. A person does not make himself, but is already largely made by the time he reaches adulthood. In that case, why should it be supposed that persons own themselves? Would it not be more reasonable to suppose that each person is equal joint owner, along with everyone else, of all persons? True, one might suppose that the equal joint owners would decide that a considerable degree of autonomous control should be 'leased back' to individuals, but this would not affect the point that ultimately proper control of each person resided in the community as a whole. In important cases, at least, some degree of control might then be imposed legitimately by the community on the talents of its members.

This view apparently presupposes a labour-mixing argument for property rights. It is not necessary, however, to consider the plausibility of such an argument. For even if we grant that those who have 'made' the present generation what they are share property rights in those persons, no justification for the equal joint ownership by the living of all the living follows. For one thing, the inherited language, customs, and cultural traditions which make us what we are were not made wholly by the previous generation, but to a large extent by persons long since dead. It would be these persons who, on the justification provided, should share ownership of us. And again, this argument would not justify our contemporaries or those who are younger than us sharing control in us, as they have had little effect (in the way here being considered) on what we have become. Only those members of previous generations who are still alive could reasonably claim a share in the ownership of others on this ground.

The end of the quest?

It may seem to be a problem with my defence of liberalism that it justifies liberal rights only so long as the quest for what is worth while in itself is unsuccessful, or at least, incomplete.[12] It is possible that a community in which all enjoy the liberal rights will reach a widespread consensus that certain things are worth while in themselves. This would not make the possession of those rights redundant, however, any more than the fact that there was widespread agreement on a certain hypothesis in physics would make the intellectual freedom of physicists redundant. For each new generation will have to accept freely for itself that the beliefs of its predecessors as to what is worth while are true. One would not wish the beliefs of later generations to represent no more than inherited dogma. But apart from that it would be extraordinary to suppose that the process of discerning what is worth while in itself could be completed. It is true that we think that some discoveries have been made, and that it is scarcely conceivable that at some later time it will be thought that these beliefs are mistaken. But there is no reason to suppose that there will ever be a point at which we can know that nothing more is to be added to the discoveries that have already been made.

In this chapter I hope to have established a consequentialist ground, and a distinctively liberal ground (though not the only ground) for assigning rights of self-ownership: that they are required in order that we can reach more reasonable views about what is worth while in itself.

4
Property

There would seem to be little point in defending people's rights of self-ownership unless one defends their rights to control things external to themselves as well. There are few, if any, activities people can engage in without making use of, or exercising control over, some portion of the material world external to themselves. Even contemplation requires that one should have the right to be where one is contemplating.[1] So there might seem to be little point in assigning individuals rights of control over their persons if they lacked rights of control over some portion of the material world. What would be the point of assigning to individuals rights protective of their choices if they lacked any rights of control over the material world external to their bodies? It would be impossible to execute most choices, and this would eliminate experimentation with different 'modes of existence'.[2]

Further, it may be noted that in several cases we could not strictly derive a characteristic set of liberal freedoms from rights of self-ownership alone. We would, as well, have to make assumptions about people's rights to make use of things external to themselves. Of Mill's freedoms, liberty of thought and feeling, and freedom of opinion and sentiment on all subjects, do not require the right to make use of external material things, other than the right to be some-where. But the freedom to express and to publish opinions does, except for directly expressing opinions to others orally, and the freedom to unite for any purpose not involving harm to others presupposes the right to be in suitable meeting places. Freedom of movement (which is not mentioned by Mill as such), obviously requires the right to make use of rights of way.

Now it might be said that this line of thought, while showing that individuals need rights of control over external material things as well as rights of self-ownership, does not show that individuals need private-property rights. It is true that in the case of some of these freedoms private-property rights would be undesirable. If all land were privately owned, then no one would have freedom of movement, except on his own land (if he owned some). The right to move to other places would be conditional upon obtaining the consent of all the owners of the land through which one passed. It would therefore seem that the land needed for rights of way should not be anyone's private property.

Notwithstanding the truth of this, there is a case for individual private-property rights, at least in some things, from the point of view of my defence of liberalism. If any individual is to have a right to make use of something as the result of the exercise of collective-ownership rights, then consent has to be obtained from the collective owners. (It may be necessary to secure the consent of all other joint owners, or of a majority of others, depending on the conception of collective ownership in operation.) Therefore individuals cannot, on their own initiative, experiment with 'modes of existence' involving use of that property, and this can be expected to inhibit such experimentation compared with a system allowing for individual private property.[3]

However, there is another argument which appears to threaten this case for an assignment of private-property rights on the basis of my justification of liberalism. Let us suppose each person is assigned private-property rights over some portion of the material world. There is a prima-facie case for any initial distribution being equal, on the assumption that there is no reason for supposing in advance that any one person's views about which activities are valuable are better than any other's. (We shall pass over certain difficulties about what would be an 'equal' initial distribution, given that there is a variety of resources to be distributed, and that there may be no established market value for resources of various kinds.) Now if the rights assigned to individuals over their initial shares are private-property rights, it follows that who has private-property rights in what particular things can be changed by mutual agreement between owners. As sequences of such transactions occur it is possible (indeed probable, given the inequalities of persons in talent, luck, and prudence) that some people will come to have property rights in more extensive material possessions than others, and that this situation will be, as Nozick has taught us, entirely in keeping with everyone's rights.[4] Such inequality is not a necessary implication of the entitlement theory. Whether it occurs depends on how, in fact, the transfers go; but its occurrence is likely enough to merit consideration.

Now a situation in which some have rights of control over extensive material possessions while others have rights over little or nothing would seem quite unsatisfactory from the viewpoint of my defence of liberalism. Consider the position of those who, as a result of a sequence of transactions, have ended up with rights over few or no material things. Earlier it was argued that to assign persons rights of self-ownership while denying them the right as individuals to control portions of the material world would defeat the point of the orginal assignment of rights of self-ownership. But a person who, as the upshot of a sequence of transactions, has property rights over little or nothing is in just that position. Though such persons may have wished to engage in certain activities, they may be unable to do so through lack of rights over appropriate material things. This renders the judgements about what is worth while of a person in such a position inoperative. This points to some qualifications of private-property rights (say through redistribution) so that no person lacks the right to control some portion of the material world.

It may be noticed that an argument for private-property rights based on an appeal to the moral value of individual autonomy would be open to a similar objection. An argument based on an appeal to autonomy would appear to provide a plausible ground for private-property rights in so far as such rights secure the things owned. But this consideration provides a case for every person capable of autonomous choice having some material things to control, for otherwise a person's autonomy is denied a certain form of expression. But under a system in which individual rights of control are determined exclusively by private-property rights, there is no guarantee that everyone would be entitled to control over at least some material things. (My basis for justifying liberalism is distinct from the appeal to the intrinsic value of individual autonomy. In my view individual autonomy indeed is of value, but as a means to more reasonable views about what is worth while in itself.)

Robert Nozick entitles a famous section of *Anarchy, State, and Utopia* 'How Liberty Upsets Patterns'.[5] The title gives the impression that the section will show how any requirement (put forward in the name of justice) which restricts or modifies private-property rights will also be an infringement of people's liberty. Now it is necessarily true that any such restriction is always an infringement of one particular liberty: the liberty of owners to do as they wish with their property. But upholding everyone's property rights may also result in certain restrictions on people's liberty, as has just been shown. And Nozick gives no argument for supposing that these restrictions matter less than the restrictions on the liberties of owners as owners.

A private-property system establishes a certain network of liberty and absences of liberty. Every owner is at liberty to control what he owns. This liberty excludes the liberty of everyone apart from the owner to control what the owner has, without his consent. Now suppose ownership rights are qualified by redistribution so as to ensure that everyone is entitled to some portion of the material world. Now there will be a different network of liberty and absences of liberty.

But nothing can be concluded from this about whether the position before redistribution is better or worse, in terms of liberty, than the position after.[6]

There is another consideration tending to the same concern about an unqualified assignment of private-property rights. My consequentialist case for assigning rights of self-ownership was that this goes some way towards ensuring that each individaul can choose what activities to engage in. Now people need to acquire rights in sufficient things to meet at least their minimal needs as well as those things necessary for pursuing such activities as they may consider valuable. If others have rights of control over what *P* needs, they may be prepared to transfer rights of control over them to *P* only if, in return, *P* agrees to give some of his time to working for them; *P* may exchange rights of control over himself, over his mental and physical powers, for agreed periods. (While universal rights of self-ownership are incompatible with involuntary slavery, they are consistent with voluntary wage labour.) Thus *P* may spend some of his time engaging in activities he considers to be of no value in themselves, and which others may control, presumably in accordance with their conception of what is worth while, not *P*'s. It is clear that a private-property system can and does create vast differences between people in the extent to which their activities are subject to the direction of others. But there is no obvious reason, in terms of my main argument for liberalism, why what might be called people's 'effective' autonomy should differ to this extent and for this reason. Why should those who happen to be in a stronger position in the market be likely to make better judgements about what activities are valuable or worth while?

To summarize: it appears that rights of self-ownership would be curtailed severely in practice if persons were not permitted, as individuals, to exercise strong rights of control over some material posessions. It also appears possible, even likely, that if a 'pure' system of private-property rights were adopted, some would come to be in a better position for expressing their choices about which activities are more

worth while than others: indeed some may have no opportunity for expressing their choices at all. In the light of this,
what view is implied by my theory of the rights of control
over material things people ought to enjoy?

While it is not my intention to pursue a utilitarian
approach, it will be inappropriate to propose a more exact
solution to our problem if any significant consequentialist
consideration is relevant to its solution. Such a consideration is relevant from the point of view of my approach to
justifying liberalism. It has been argued that persons ought
to be assigned certain rights to enable them to choose freely
which activities they consider to be most worth while. This
may not seem to have much to do with the circumstances in
which most people find themselves; most people not having
the opportunity to pursue any view of what is worth while in
itself. What are the main limitations on people exploring
their conceptions of what is worth while in itself? Most
people have to spend a substantial proportion of their lives
in occupations from which they derive their material
support. Mostly they regard these occupations as of wholly
instrumental value: if it were not economically necessary to
follow them, people would not engage in them. These
occupations leave little time and energy for the pursuit of
things worth while to themselves. And the economic return
from most occupations does not leave much in the way of
resources for the pursuit of what is worth while in itself,
once essential needs have been met. Therefore a criterion
emerges for judging any system of rights of control over
material things. To what extent will a given system of rights
of control have a long-run tendency to relieve people of
'economic necessity': to relieve them of engaging in activities
they consider to be wholly of instrumental value, and to
provide them with adequate resources for the pursuit of
what they consider to be worth while in itself?

To take this point further we must clarify the ideas of
engaging in an activity for instrumental and for non-
instrumental reasons. To say that person *P* engages in
activity *A* for reasons he believes to be wholly instrumental

is to say that he engages in *A only* because he believes that doing so will produce some result, *R*, he wants. Therefore if *P* came to believe either that

1 he didn't want *R* any more; or that
2 engaging in *A* does not bring the result *R*; or that
3 engaging in another activity, *B*, is, *ceteris paribus*, a better way of securing *R*,

then *P* would consider himself no longer to have reason for engaging in *A*. By contrast, to say that *P* believes that *A* is not wholly of instrumental value implies that *P* would consider himself to have reason to engage in *A* even if one or more of (1), (2) and (3) held.

This is a formal account of what it is for *P* to believe that an activity is to be engaged in for wholly instrumental reasons. I will not attempt to say which activities are properly to be engaged in for wholly instrumental reasons, though some of my own assumptions will be apparent in examples. This is because people differ not only on whether an activity is intrinsically valuable, where all are agreed that if it were valuable at all it would be intrinsically valuable, but also on whether the value of something is or is not wholly instrumental value. Opinions change on whether activities or things are to be judged within the instrumental or intrinsic category. The spinning wheel, once judged from the point of view of its effCiency for spinning, is now judged as an item of cottage decor. Or the once admired piece of tourist kitsch is now judged from the point of view of whether it is heavy enough to keep the door open. If the question of what is of intrinsic value is open then, to some extent, the question of whether some things are only of instrumental value must also be kept open.

Nevertheless there is considerable agreement in practice that certain activities are wholly of instrumental value. If the quality of dental health now achieved by dentistry could be achieved by some much less time-consuming process, we would not expect many people to think that there was still reason to practise dentistry. (However if some people, who

knew about the less time-consuming process, still wished to
go to dentists, it would not be permissible to prevent them,
for their wish presumably would indicate that they thought
going to the dentist not wholly of instrumental value.) Now
my approach to justifying liberalism suggests that it is
choices between activities considered to be not wholly of
instrumental value that are significant. Therefore a criterion
emerges for preferring one economic system to another,
which may be illustrated by this example. Suppose the total
amount of salt desired by everyone for culinary purposes
is S. Method $M1$ of producing S requires p persons
to work h hours. Method $M2$ requires less than ph man
hours to produce S. Everyone regards the activities involved
in $M1$ and $M2$ as of wholly instrumental value. We shall call
$M2$ a 'more efficient' way of producing S than $M1$. What
makes the second case more efficient is that less labour
(regarded by those who perform the labour as wholly of
instrumental value) is necessary to produce the same result.
It is irrelevant whether the result produced is regarded as of
instrumental or non-instrumental value, though in the
present example the result would be likely to be regarded as
itself of instrumental value. From the point of view of my
overall approach a more efficient economy (in this sense of
'more efficient') is to be preferred. The less persons have to
spend their time in activities they consider to be of wholly
instrumental value the better.

My use of 'efficiency' in this way is non-standard. As it is a
term which (with a different meaning) is favoured by those
with views very different from mine, it is worth making the
distinction. An improvement in 'efficiency', as that term is
often used by those who call for 'greater economic efficiency', means that goods or services of a given market value
are now produced at a lower cost than they were at a
previous time. I shall call this the 'conservative' definition of
efficiency. Some cases where, on my meaning, greater
efficiency has come about would not count as greater
efficiency on the conservative view. Suppose dental services
were rendered obsolete by the addition of trace elements to

the water supply. This would not be a more (conservative) efficient provision of dental services, as no dental services are now supplied; but given that everyone regards dental services as of wholly instrumental value, the economy has become more efficient on my view, *ceteris paribus*.

It is commonly claimed by conservatives that a system of minimally constrained private-property rights tends to maximize economic efficiency. Even if this is true, it will only have been shown that such a system maximizes 'conservative' efficiency. Such arguments do not show that a *laissez-faire* system maximizes efficiency in the sense that is important from a liberal point of view. For example, under a *laissez-faire* system some established producers might succeed in persuading consumers to continue to buy goods of only instrumental value which it was in fact no longer necessary for consumers to have because the same end could be better achieved in another way. If such persuasion were successful, the economy would be made less efficient in my meaning (everything else remaining the same).

Further, suppose the aggregate market value of dental services had been considerable, while the market value of trace elements added to the water supply is very little. Other things remaining the same, the GNP per caput will have declined. From the liberal point of view therefore, economic progress does not necessarily involve a rising GNP per caput.

It is plausible that the factor I have attempted to isolate and refer to as 'efficiency' is affected by the system of rights of control over material things which prevails. The extent to which it is affected by various systems of rights of control surely cannot be determined without empirical investigation. Therefore there is an aspect of the answer to the question 'What system of rights of control over material things is required by my approach?' which can be taken no further by purely philosophical methods. This is not to deny that philosophical distinctions may be relevant to such research. For example, we may distinguish between the 'structure' of a system of rights of control, such as Nozick's

entitlement theory, and the economic 'formations' which
are compatible with the structure, though not required by it.
The family business, the multinational corporation, and the
voluntary co-operative are all consistent with the entitlement theory (if they have arisen by legitimate processes).
None of them is required by it, and any of them may or may
not be a significant feature of an economic scene over which
the entitlement conception prevails. Now it may be difficult
to discover to what extent efficiency is influenced by the
structure of a system of rights of control, and to what extent
it is influenced by the particular economic formations which
happen to be significant at a particular time within that
structure.

There appears to be a problem about this approach to
liberalism and property rights, however. It is said that there
is an appropriate goal by which to judge any system of rights
of control over material things. It is 'To what extent does
that system, in the long term, tend to reduce economic
necessity in aggregate?' Now to be tied down by economic
necessity is to be tied down by productive activity one
regards as of wholly instrumental value. A problem might
be thought to arise due to my refusal to give anything but a
'formal' criterion for distinguishing 'wholly instrumental
activity' from 'not wholly instrumental activity'. No resort
has been made to 'objective' principles by which an activity
of this or that kind (for example, digging holes in the road)
can be conclusively characterized as 'wholly instrumental'.
If that is so, it may be asked how we can arrive at any
decisions about when wholly instrumental activity has been
reduced. From the point of view of person A the elimination
of job J may be the elimination of a job which was wholly of
instrumental value, and therefore a contribution to the
reduction of economic necessity. But from the point of view
of B the elimination of J may be the loss of something not
wholly of instrumental value: it may be the loss of something
which, at least in part, was worth while in itself.

To be applicable, the view put forward about liberalism
and property rights presupposes that there are substantial

areas of agreement that certain activities are wholly of instrumental value. But it is not unreasonable to expect that there will be this agreement. For example, electric lighting eliminated the need for gas-lamp lighters; the automatic telephone exchange eliminated the need for many manual telephone operators, and I would not expect many to regard these occupations as of anything but wholly instrumental value. It is not denied, of course, that there will be cases of serious disagreement, but this does not matter, provided there is a sufficient area of agreement for the criterion to be applicable.

Liberalism and capitalism

My conception of a proper objective of an economic system is similar to that advocated by G. A. Cohen.[7] He favours as an objective increases in 'leisure', roughly defined as 'freedom from unappealing activity'; and reduction in 'toil' – 'unappealing' activity. 'Leisure' as so defined is not necessarily not gainful employment, and not necessarily not strenuous, and 'time off' is not necessarily not devoted to toil (*Marx*, p. 304). It may be that there is a difference of emphasis in the reasons for which he and I accept relief from economic necessity as desirable. Cohen is apt to characterize the value of relief from economic necessity in neo-hedonistic terms: 'freedom from *unappealing* activity', and from '*unwanted* activity' (*Marx*, p. 323), while for me its value lies in the freedom of persons to pursue their conceptions of what is worth while in itself. In general such pursuit no doubt will be appealing, but its value is not seen as wholly constituted by its being pleasurable, and sometimes it may be disagreeable. Nevertheless the differences in our respective goals are not significant for the subsequent discussion. His emphasis in *Shmoo* on leisure as an opportunity for people to develop their talents and lead worth while lives brings our conceptions of the goal even closer.

In *Shmoo* Cohen allows that capitalism has developed 'a

superb technology which could be used to restrict unwanted labour to a modest place in life'. But the potential this technology provides for allowing people to develop and exercise their talents is not realised under capitalism. For the opportunity to develop one's talents requires leisure, or at least release from most existing jobs, as 'for most people what they have to do to earn a living isn't a source of joy.' Now the improved productivity capitalism provides may be taken in increased leisure, output remaining constant, or in increased output with no increase in leisure, or in some mixture of both. Cohen claims that capitalism will favour increased output with no increase in leisure, or if no expansion of the market for an existing product is possible, then introduction into the market of new products, as this is the strategy favourable to maximizing profits. Thus the leisure capitalism could have provided for developing people's talents will not be realized. There will be, instead, 'an endless chase after consumer goods'. Capitalism is self-defeating: it creates the potential for people to have more leisure in which to develop their talents and lead more worthwhile lives, but then frustrates that potential, by encouraging people to consume more goods, and hence continue in productive activity they regard as of only instrumental value.

The productive technology of advanced capitalism begets an unparalleled opportunity of lifting the curse of Adam and liberating men from toil, but the production relations of capitalist economic organization prevent the opportunity from being seized. The economic form most able to relieve toil is least disposed to do so. (*Marx*, p. 306)

To date I have been somewhat agnostic concerning what actual system of rights of control might be best justified in terms of the reduction of economic necessity. However, if Cohen is correct the acceptance of the reduction of economic necessity as a goal implies a much more definite view than has so far been stated. My conception of liberalism would imply the rejection of capitalism. From the point of view of my justification of liberalism, is this a conclusive reason for rejecting capitalism? I have refused to put forward any supposedly 'objective' criterion for what is and what is not wholly of instrumental value. It is up to people to choose for themselves what is wholly of instrumental value, and what is wholly or partly of value in itself. Is that consistent with the view, apparently presupposed in Cohen's criticism of capitalism, that it is in some sense 'irrational' (beyond a certain point) to be persuaded to sacrifice leisure for more consumption?

Let us consider the story of the unrepentant Yuppy. A Yuppy works very hard at a job he regards as of only instrumental value, thereby making a packet, which he spends on all kinds of consumer goods. Cohen offers him the option of working fewer hours at the same job and earning less, or alternatively, a job the Yuppy would find interesting to do, but which pays less. In other words, the Yuppy is offered less purely instrumental activity, but also fewer consumer goods. The Yuppy says he would sooner stay with his high-paying job. Can we show the Yuppy that this choice is in some way irrational?

Perhaps we can show the Yuppy that it is irrational to want all these consumer goods. Consider this top-of-the-market dishwasher. We say that it is irrational for him to buy this dishwasher because all that he wants a dishwasher to do can be done by this simpler one at half the price. We assume that any reasonable person only buys a dishwasher for what a dishwasher can do. But the Yuppy says 'I simply want the best on the market.' Can we say 'It is irrational of you to want a dishwasher for that kind of reason'? If I do not want to advance any supposedly 'objective' criterion for what is and is not of wholly instrumental value, I cannot say that the Yuppy is wrong to think that it is desirable to have a top-of-the-market dishwasher for this reason. Now this might seem to pose a problem for my conception of liberalism as well as for Cohen's conception of socialism. What if the Yuppy ideology spreads to just about everyone,

and nearly all are working very hard at jobs they regard as of
purely instrumental value, but contentedly, because they
can have ever more (and more elaborate) consumer goods?

It would still be true that members of this Yuppy society
would have reason to prefer less to more instrumental
activity to attain a given end. So my notion of 'relief from
economic necessity' is still applicable. What concerns us is
the conception of what is worth while in itself accepted in
this society, which is hardly what Mill would have hoped for.
I have denied myself an appeal to objective criteria by which
it is determined what is worth while in itself, and by
reference to which it can be said that in the Yuppy society
we have a mistake about what is worth while in itself.
Nevertheless there is a sense in which we might still believe
this to be a mistake. In the past certain ways of living have
been accepted as worth while, and later come to have been
rejected as valueless. For example, the insistence on
elaborate manners and dress amongst the eighteenth-
century European aristocracy struck the French revolu-
tionaries, and strikes us, as ridiculous. Similarly we might
expect that, at least in the long run, the view of the Yuppy
society as to what is worth while in itself would not prevail.
So I think Cohen's case against capitalism would still hold,
so far as this objection is concerned, if we have certain
beliefs about what, in the long term, people will regard as
worth while in itself.

But there is another objection to Cohen's case. It has
already been pointed out that societies which have private-
property rights as the basic legal form of control over
material things can vary considerably in respect of the form
of economic organization which is predominant. In
eighteenth-century England it was the large estate, in the
late nineteenth century the family firm, and in the twentieth
century it is the multinational corporation. Capitalism is a
particular form of economic organization possible under a
system of private-property rights. According to Cohen, the
distinctive characteristic of capitalism is that economic
activity is undertaken in order to increase exchange value,

which may take the form either of profit or of growth (*Marx*, p. 302). (I shall not express a view on whether this is an appropriate definition of capitalism. The subsequent argument is relative to Cohen's definition, and therefore might not apply if other definitions were preferred.) Many forms of economic activity existing in capitalist societies are not, on this definition therefore, 'capitalist': private universities, for example. They operate within the legal structure of a private-property system in that they own premises and equipment, 'market' products, receive payment for them, and pay employees, but they would not on the present definition count as capitalist organizations because increasing exchange value (as distinct from 'paying their way') is not an objective of these undertakings.

If a capitalist system has provided sufficient relief from economic necessity, there may be many non-capitalist enterprises for which profit is not a significant consideration. We might hope that both the producers and the consumers of such organizations find what they do to be of worth for its own sake. And this is already often the case with private schools and universities, some sports organizations, theatre, orchestral, ballet, and opera groups; charities, religious organizations, museums, and art galleries. There are also many small private businesses, for example in bookselling and the making of craft and art objects, in which proprietors are not primarily interested in profits. No doubt capitalist firms will attempt to resist the emigration of workers and consumers to such organizations; that is, resist the eventual relegation of capitalist firms to a minor part of the economy, for this process would undermine the importance, wealth, and power of capitalist firms. But there is no reason why such resistance must be successful. It has happened before that once economically powerful groups within a private-property system (e.g. the British landed aristocracy in the first part of the nineteenth century) have, despite resistance, declined.

To this it may be replied (as Cohen suggests in *Shmoo*) that 'the capitalist system operates to ensure that people's desire for goods is never satisfied.' Capitalist firms will attempt to encourage either increased consumption of the same goods, or else initiate consumption of new goods. We do not know whether this is a process which can be made to continue indefinitely, or whether some 'natural' limit of consumption of goods and services will be reached (i.e. of goods and services wanted for wholly instrumental reasons). It is not obvious that no such limit exists. We have, and often apply to our own behaviour, a notion of 'irrational' consumption, i.e. consumption which is not of either instrumental or non-instrumental value. It is not clear why capitalist firms should always be able to override the promptings of this thought.

We may now draw some conclusions about the relationship between my conception of liberalism and capitalism.

1 In so far as capitalism has a tendency to increase productivity it is desirable, in that it (at least potentially) reduces the sphere of 'economic necessity'.
2 In so far as capitalism has a tendency to the indiscriminate encouragement of consumption, irrespective of its instrumental or non-instrumental desirability, it is deplorable.
3 In so far as capitalism is apt to adopt productive methods that, from the point of view of the producers, are merely instrumentally desirable, capitalism is deplorable.

Regarding (1), (2) and (3) there is no disagreement with Cohen. He draws these further conclusions.

(a) Capitalism is now a system of net disadvantage from the point of view of reducing economic necessity, because any remaining advantages under (1) are now outweighed by the combined disadvantages of (2) and (3).
(b) Therefore capitalism is to be rejected *in toto*, along with private property (anyway in the means of production). In *Shmoo* Cohen recommends that we share our material resources and take the leisure we can have with existing technology, rather than pursuing the produc-

tion of ever more goods and services. We should 'restrict unwanted labour to a modest place in life.'

My view is that there is no call to take a stand on whether capitalism is now a system of net disadvantage from the point of view of relieving economic necessity. There is no need to raise the question whether capitalism is to be wholly accepted or wholly rejected. In some areas capitalism may still be able to contribute further to the reduction of 'economic necessity'. It is possible for consumers to resist the pressure to indulge in pointless consumption. In so far as such resistance occurs, the capitalist firm will take a declining share of the economy. The question whether capitalism is to be rejected (in whole or in part) is not the same issue as whether private property in the means of production is to be rejected. Capitalism could be wholly or partly dispensed with while private-property rights remained the dominant form of control over material things. Therefore there is no obvious argument to a socialist economy from the acceptance of (1), (2) and (3). The acceptance of the goal of relief from economic necessity does not imply (total) rejection of capitalism or private property. This argument is only intended to show that my conception of liberalism does not imply the rejection of capitalism *for these reasons Cohen gives for rejecting capitalism*. It could still be true that, on the basis of the empirical evidence, my position implies the rejection of capitalism.

Provisos

So, is the general form of a solution to the problem of what implications my conception of liberalism has for property rights to be stated as follows: 'Choose that system of rights of control over material things which it is reasonable to believe, on the basis of the evidence, will maximize increases in efficiency'? This answer will have to be qualified on a number of counts.

For this principle to be applicable it must be assumed that there is at least one system of rights of control over material things which, if in operation, would contribute to the relief of economic necessity. To advance this principle it is necessary to have at least this degree of optimism. The principle would be inapplicable if circumstances were such that no member of the set of possible systems of rights of control over material things would produce any relief from economic necessity. The principle could be restated to take account of those with a pessimistic outlook as follows: 'Choose that system of rights of control over material things which it is reasonable to believe, on the basis of the evidence, will either maximize efficiency or minimize the reduction of efficiency.'[8]

This principle is not to be regarded as the only consideration determining what system of rights of control over material things there should be. In so far as this discussion of property can be regarded as a contribution to a comprehensive account of distributive justice, it is to be seen as only one ingredient in such an account. The best-known contemporary theories of distributive justice, those of Rawls and Nozick, attempt to give a complete account of what is distributively just, in the sense of purporting to capture within their respective principles every significant normative consideratiion that is involved in the determination of what is just. The present discussion is not an attempt at comprehensiveness. My defence of liberalism has certain implications for property rights, but it would be absurd to claim that these implications are the only considerations involved in an account of distributive justice. People's needs are obviously a further consideration, and so is the question of whether a society could be expected to be stable in the long term with a given distribution of rights. The basis of the present account of property rights (and of rights of self-ownership) is how people can come to have more reasonable views about what is worth while in itself. People are also concerned, and in unfavourable circumstances largely preoccupied with, their material needs. While it may be true that satisfying these needs is a 'mere means' to other aspirations, in sufficiently urgent circumstances the provision of 'mere means' will be much more important than the possession of what is worth while in itself.

Even if we set aside considerations of distributive justice external to my account of liberalism, there are still reasons for further modifying the principle given. The system of rights of control over material things which maximizes efficiency might be such that some come to be not entitled to any material things at all. It is conceivable, for example, that the system which maximizes 'efficiency' is the entitlement conception. It has already been argued that such a situation would be unsatisfactory from the point of view of my justification of liberalism. Those who lack rights to any material things are unable to engage in activities they consider to be worth while in themselves.

If the system of rights of control which maximized efficiency had the effect that some lacked rights of control over any material things, on what basis should the system which maximizes efficiency be modified? Several of these bases would be external to my conception of liberalism: for example, the satisfaction of certain needs. But a basis internal to my conception of liberalism can be discerned also. Suppose the system of rights of control over material things optimal in terms of efficiency is private-property rights. A basis for redistribution internal to my conception of liberalism would be to redistribute to those who lacked sufficient resources to pursue their conceptions of what is worth while. In doing this we have to accept, at least provisionally, current orthodoxy about which activities are worth while in themselves, and redistribute to those who wish to pursue these activities, giving preference to those who show most promise of pursuing them well, until the resources available for redistribution are exhausted. But is this use of current norms arbitrary in terms of the view that a justification for a liberal set of individual rights is to be found in terms of the search for that which is desirable in itself? It would be inconsistent with this view to say that any

conception of what is desirable in itself is wholly characterized by reference to the norms of some particular culture,
for then the possibilities of 'exploration' would be very
limited. But this is not required for the position proposed:
what is required is the different view that in order to defend
a claim that something is desirable in itself against the
sceptical we have no starting-point other than what is
currently recognized as such within a certain culture. A
defence, by way of showing resemblences, may be available
in one culture, though not in another, and to that extent a
relativistic approach is plausible. In view of this consideration, it is not arbitrary to distribute surplus resources by
reference to current norms of what is desirable in itself.

The idea of equality of opportunity can be seen from this
point of view also. Equality of opportunity may be 'formal',
i.e. people are barred from the opportunity to seek some
good only because of characteristics relevant to the pursuit
or enjoyment of the good. Or it may be 'substantial', i.e.
people are, as much as human effort and organization will
allow, given an equal chance of actually gaining the goods in
question (barring 'natural' differences in talent, and 'moral'
differences). In the latter case it can only be determined
whether people have enjoyed equality of opportunity if
there is a consensus as to what constitutes a valued
opportunity. Standardly those who press for 'substantial'
equality of opportunity assume that there is a consensus:
that the goods in question are status, wealth, and power,
and what in a particular society can be expected to be means
to these goods. My conception of liberalism is reserved
about equality of opportunity in this sense, because it
presupposes a definite, conventional, and dubious conception of what is to be valued. But equality of opportunity to
become acquainted with the cultural tradition of one's
community is desirable (though not merely as a means to
personal advancement).[9]

This consideration may do something to reduce the
inequalities between members of a given generation in the
enjoyment of freedom from economic necessity. There is a

further problem of justice, however: that between members of present and future generations. Rights of control over material things are to be organized so as to maximize relief from economic necessity. But might not this prove to be a 'jam tomorrow' doctrine? At time t_1 the system of rights of control which does this best may do nothing to relieve the economic necessity of the t_1 generation (G_1), even though it optimizes the prospects of subsequent generations being so relieved. For example, the system of rights of control at t_1 gives rise to a situation where everyone is engaged either in producing economic necessities, or in capital investment in technical innovation expected to relieve economic necessity for subsequent generations. All this activity is regarded by the participants as of only instrumental value. Now people prefer to do things they think are not wholly of an instrumental character. Would it be fair, then, that members of G_1 should engage almost entirely in instrumental activities, so that subsequent generations will be able to spend more of their lives in non-instrumental pursuits? This is the counterpart, for my form of consequentialist justification, to the problem of justice between generations in conventional forms of utilitarianism.

As before, there will be reasons external to my liberal justification for why earlier generations should not be sacrificed to later. But there is also a reason internal to my justification of liberalism for not wholly sacrificing present to future generations, even if this were to maximize long-term progress in efficiency. Activities thought to be worth while in themselves are in many cases the products of an intellectual or an artistic tradition. Exclusive concentration on efficiency could, in some circumstances, threaten the continuance of such traditions. It is possible, of course, that the system of rights of control which maximizes efficiency could prove to be compatible with the continuance of a certain tradition. Suppose that at t_1 the system which maximizes efficiency is *laissez-faire* capitalism. It may be that wealthy patrons voluntarily transfer sufficient resources for various traditions to flourish. But there is no reason to

believe that the situation always will be like this, and
therefore my underlying defence of liberalism would imply a
further modification of the efficiency doctrine. That system
of rights of control over material things which is optimal for
efficiency may have to be further modified to ensure that
there are sufficient resources for the continuance of such
traditions.

It is also a reason why a liberal society should promote the
education of its members in those activities considered to be
worth while in themselves (according to the cultural
traditions of that society). Education should not be
restricted to the skills it is anticipated will be of use for the
material support of the society. For such skills, and the
subculture surrounding the activities in which they are
deployed, become instrumentally redundant, and the
former practitioners are then often lost for some new
activity to engage in. It is the task of education not only to
impart useful skills, but to acquaint the members of a society
with as many as possible of the activities believed, at that
point in a cultural tradition, to be worth while for their own
sake.

So far we have considered what qualifications might have
to be made to a system of private-property rights, if that
proved to be the best system to have from the point of view
of relief from economic necessity. But if a system of rights of
control over material things is assessed on the basis of its
contribution to efficiency, there is no necessity that such a
system will contain private-property rights as a significant
element. It may or it may not, depending on what system in
fact contributes best to efficiency, and this, I have allowed,
is an empirical question. But should not private-property
rights be given a more secure place in my conception of
liberalism than this consideration may allow? After all, if my
ground for liberalism requires self-ownership rights, and the
exercise of self-ownership rights requires rights over
material things, it would seem that private-property rights
should be a component of any acceptable system of rights of
control. In order for there to be experiments as to what is

worth while in itself, some use of material resources will be required. If rights over material resources take the form of individual private-property rights, then one person, or a few people, may make such experiments on their own initiative. If these rights are collective, then the worth of the experiments must be justified to the collective, i.e. to conventional expectations, and interesting innovation is less likely. It would seem, therefore, that private-property rights should be an element in any system of rights of control. Therefore my position should be modified as follows. There may, or may not, be a case for private-property rights on the basis of 'efficiency'. Whatever is the position on that basis there is, additionally, a place for private-property rights from a liberal point of view because without them persons cannot effectively exercise rights of self-ownership.

One strand in the liberal tradition, the libertarian, has seen a very close connection between the liberal rights of individuals and the unqualified acceptance of private-property rights. That has always been a minority strand within the liberal tradition.[10] The view proposed here of the connection between liberalism and private-property rights lies within the majority tradition. The liberty of individuals, in the way I see that liberty as valuable, is not necessarily best served by an uncompromised system of private-property rights. It is at least possible, though I think present evidence suggests that it is unlikely, that economic 'efficiency' should be best served by a system in which private-property rights have a minor role. However I claim that upholding the liberal rights of individuals is not compatible with the entire abandonment of private-property rights.

The desirability, or otherwise, of private-property rights has been considered from the point of view of relief from economic necessity. Such relief is thought desirable because it allows people to engage in activities they believe to be at least partly of intrinsic value. But is this not to assume that everyone will consider the value of a system of private-property rights (or of an alternative system, such as collective ownership) wholly from an instrumental point of view? Is it not possible that some might regard a system of private-property rights (or an alternative system) as of intrinsic value? For example, some might regard the exercise of individual private-property rights as an aspect of the exercise of individual autonomy, which they see as of value in itself. Others might see the exercise of collective-property rights as an expression of human capacities for co-operation and mutual sympathy, and regard that as an intrinsically desirable aspect of human life. Proponents of both systems would agree that the choice of a system of rights of control over material things directly affects their opportunities for pursuing their respective conceptions of what is worth while in itself: that this choice is not neutral in its effects on their respective conceptions of what is of value.

The problem for my position is analogous to, though different from, a problem in trying to justify private-property rights (or alternative forms of rights of control) in terms of preference utilitarianism. In this case it would be quite arbitrary to exclude preferences (as such) for individual private-property rights, or for collective-property rights, in making utilitarian comparisons of these systems. It could be envisaged that in a society accustomed to private-property rights the preference for them would be strong, and similarly in a society accustomed to collective-property rights; and that these differences might weight the balance in the choice of a utilitarianly optimal system of rights. It is difficult to see how, from a preference-utilitarian point of view, any such sets of preferences could be regarded as irrational: for example, a widespread desire in a capitalist society to possess things as one's private property, even if doing so is less than optimally efficient for satisfying other desires.

Merely to have a preference for something is not the same as to regard it as worth while in itself. Even so, it would appear that someone could regard the existence of private-property rights (or of collective-ownership rights) as a state of affairs desirable in itself. If so, the discussion of this chapter would seem to be based on an unfounded assumption. I do not believe that such systems of rights of control are of worth or value in themselves, but it is doubtful whether it can be demonstrated that they are not simply by giving attention to the concept of intrinsic value.

5

Intrinsic Value

Liberalism has been characterized in terms of rights of self-ownership. Respect for those rights has been defended by showing how it is related to having more reasonable views about what is valuable in itself. To sustain such a defence of liberalism two theses about intrinsic value have to be true.

1 An 'objective' account of intrinsic value (in a sense to be explained) is not implausible.
2 We are not certain, beyond reasonable doubt, what things are of intrinsic value.

The first thesis ensures that the exploration for what is of value in itself is not futile; the second, that it is not redundant. We begin with a defence of the first thesis.

An objective account of intrinsic value

An initially attractive way of stating the objective view is to say that it asserts that claims of the form 'O has intrinsic value' are either true or false. The truth and falsity of claims about intrinsic value may be conceived in two ways. (1) Such claims may be understood by analogy with the assertion that a certain thing has a certain property, for example, 'This is yellow' is true if this has the property of being yellow. Similarly 'This is of intrinsic value' is true if this has the property of being of intrinsic value. (2) To say that something is of intrinsic value is not to claim that it has a certain property, but that it satisfies certain criteria. Kant and Hare have thought in terms of the criterial conception of goodness, while Hume and Moore have thought in terms of the property conception. The criterial form of the objective view would say that assertions of the form 'O is of intrinsic value' are true if O satisfies the criteria for something's being of intrinsic value. If we wish to say that evaluative claims can be true or false, this does not imply that we must take such claims as asserting the presence of a property: a point some moral realists appear to ignore.[1]

It is not enough, however, for characterizing the objective view to say that it claims that assertions of the form 'O is of intrinsic value' are either true or false, in the property sense or in the criterial sense. Consider, for example, the 'property' of a television programme's being entertaining. So far as you are concerned it is either true or false that the programme is entertaining. But its having that property is clearly dependent on its being you, with your tastes, who is making the judgement. We are reluctant to think of the programme as, in itself, either entertaining or not entertaining. While we can speak of such a judgement as being either true or false, it is clear that it is also subject dependent. The same consideration applies in the case of the criterial conception. For dog-show enthusiasts it is true that this poodle is a good poodle if it measures up well to the criteria used by dog-show enthusiasts for poodles being good ones, but this judgement is dependent upon a certain group happening to use certain criteria for judging a certain kind of dog. In both cases it seems reasonable to say that the judgements can be true or false, but also, that they are subject dependent.[2]

Thus a more satisfactory formulation of the objective position contains two elements.

(1) Assertions of the form '*O* has intrinsic value' are true or false.
(2) The truth or falsity of such assertions is not subject dependent.

This position can take a 'property' or 'criterial' form. In the property form it is claimed that the truth or falsity of '*O* has intrinsic value' depends on the possession of a non-subject-dependent property of intrinsic value. In the criterial form the truth or falsity of '*O* has intrinsic value' depends on a thing's satisfying non-subject-dependent criteria for the presence of intrinsic value.

It may be noticed that these points about the relationships between objectivity, truth and falsity, and subject dependence also have application to something's being of extrinsic value. If being 'objectively' good only requires that statements concerning goodness can be true or false, then claims that things have extrinsic value can be objective. If this chair can be used to stand on so as to reach the high shelf, then it is true that it is good for this purpose. But if being 'objectively' good is taken to imply a denial of subject dependence, then the chair's being good is not an objective matter, for it depends upon some agent (or agents) having appropriate purposes and being in an appropriate situation.

Turning now to the subjective view, it similarly should be stated in terms of an assertion of the subject dependence of claims about intrinsic value, rather than in terms of a denial of their truth or falsity. In the property form, the subjective view says that our beliefs that some things possess a property of intrinsic value are subject dependent. A well-known variant of this view, endorsed by Mackie,[3] goes like this. Suppose you believe that *O* is of intrinsic value. What you believe indeed is that *O* possesses a property of a certain kind. However, *O* does not in fact possess such a property, nor is it possible that it could. The properties *O* really does possess, in conjunction with your perceptual and psychological apparatus, give rise to certain affective states of mind. These states cause you to project a property on to *O*, which you suppose O to have. Now if O has a certain set of qualities such that a certain group of persons all react to O by attributing to it possession of a property of intrinsic value, we might allow that it is true that it has that property (for that group of persons). The real thrust of the subjective view is its assertion of subject dependence: nothing could be of intrinsic value unless there were beings with certain perceptual and psychological capacities.

There are also criterial versions of the subjective view. According to them, when we judge something to be of intrinsic value, we are judging that it measures up to certain criteria. The crucial point is not so much whether claims about intrinsic value can be true or false, but rather whether the criteria have a subject-dependent status. Relativism, for example, is not out to contest the applicability of the notions of truth and falsity, but rather to insist upon the relativity of the criteria by reference to which those notions are applied.

In what follows only the property versions of the subjective and objective views will be considered. The reason for this is the implausibility of a criterial approach to what is of intrinsic value. We may take, as an example, Nozick's view[4] that 'the basic dimension of intrinsic value is degree of organic unity.' Putting aside the problems of knowing how to apply such a criterion, it is clear that, even if everything we believed to be of intrinsic value did manifest a high degree of organic unity, it would not be because we recognised that something did that we would be convinced it was of intrinsic value. The judgement that some particular thing is of intrinsic value would be primary, and generalisations about the characteristics possessed by all things of intrinsic value (if such could be found) would have only a derivative status. Our judgements would not depend on the criteria: the criteria would arise from our confident judgements.

I take it that the subjective view is currently the favoured position, and that it is only if some dissatisfaction with it can be elicited that any need will be felt to formulate a plausible version of an objective view. The first of the difficulties with the subjective view is that it is not, strictly speaking, an account of intrinsic value at all. According to G. E. Moore, 'To say that a kind of value is "intrinsic" means merely that the question whether a thing possesses it, and in what degree it possesses it, depends solely on the intrinsic nature of the thing in question.'[5] The value of something that has intrinsic value is non-relational. If P believes that O is of intrinsic value, then P's belief does not depend, epistemically or causally, upon P's beliefs about how O is in fact related to other things P believes to be of value. For example, P believes that this chair is of value because he can stand on it to reach things from the high shelf, and P wants to get things from the high shelf. If P were no longer to believe that the chair was of value, were he to cease to believe it could be used to get things from the high shelf, or if he were no longer to want to get things from the high shelf, then the value P believes the chair to have would be extrinsic. But if P were to believe that the chair was of value, no matter what changes there were in P's beliefs about how the chair is related to other things, and no matter what changes there were in P's wants, then P would believe that the chair has intrinsic value. In this case P might regard the chair as, in effect, a sculpture, as some regard a de Stijl chair.[6] A belief that O has intrinsic value is not affected by changes in beliefs about how O is related to other things, or by changes in beliefs about what other things are of value.

A belief that something is of intrinsic value is non-relational in a further sense. While all cases where O is believed to be of intrinsic value are cases where the value of O is seen as not dependent on the value of anything else, not all cases where the value of O is seen as not dependent on the value of something else are cases of intrinsic value. Consider the value someone finds in relaxation after a period of sustained work. This person need not see the value of relaxation as extrinsic as, say, would someone who thought 'I must relax now if I am to do well in the exam.' But the value relaxation seems to have may be dependent on context: if he had not been working hard he may not have seen relaxation as attractive in itself. In this case the value of relaxation, though not extrinsic, is not intrinsic either.

Now it is an implication of the subjective view that the value anything has is not due solely to the properties it possesses, but is due as well to states of mind produced in those who have experience of that thing. It follows that on the subjective view nothing has intrinsic value. And this is not because there could have been things of intrinsic value, but none such exists; but because it is not possible that there should be anything of intrinsic value. At least one proponent of the subjective view, Mackie, does accept that nothing has intrinsic value: we only believe that some things are of intrinsic value.[7] All these beliefs are, strictly, false, so the subjective view needs to be supplemented by an 'error theory'; an explanation of why it should seem that some things have value of a kind that they could not possibly have. Strictly there could not be a subjective view of intrinsic value, but rather a subjective account of our beliefs that certain things have intrinsic value.

The second difficulty arises from reflection on the phenomenology of our judgements that things have intrinsic value. Suppose that you have been moved by a good performance of *Tosca*, and believe you have encountered something good in itself, and not merely good for some purpose, such as exposing the evils of a police state. The situation will present itself to you as one in which you encountered something of value, and because of that you responded in a certain way. It is not that the response makes you see it as of value, but that your appreciating it for what it was, something of value, caused the response. The phenomenology of the situation suggests just the reverse account to that offered by the subjective view.

The subjective view allows that this is a correct description of our experiences of value, but insists that what is naturally suggested by the experience is not how things really are. In support it may be pointed out that we do take such a view in other areas: for example someone who believes that yellow is a secondary quality need not deny that we see things as being yellow, rather than as appearing yellow, as we do when wearing tinted glasses. The subjective view simply claims that there is an explicable error in what is suggested by the phenomenology.

A third objection to the subjective theory is based on our belief that we can make, and correct, mistakes in what we believe to be of intrinsic value. We may suppose something to be of value, but eventually come to realise that our belief was due to some factor which distorted our judgement. For example, you know that your friend thought O to be of value, and because of a wish to please your friend you too (mistakenly, as you later realized) supposed O to be of value. Or you may come to realize that you had preconceived attitudes about what could be of value (due to conventional attitudes, perhaps) which blinded you to the value something unconventional has. Now if we suppose ourselves sometimes to be misled in our affective responses, how can our beliefs that certain things are of intrinsic value themselves be due to affective responses?

A supporter of the subjective view could reply that this argument rests on the assumption that the common belief that we can make mistakes about what is of intrinsic value implies that what we are doing is making mistakes. How do we know that we are making mistakes rather than (as we would say in a matter of taste) changing our minds? The argument assumes the point at issue, it may be said. In any case the subjective view could be developed to give an account of why we should take some affective responses to be 'veridical' and others not. A suitable analogy is suggested by what we say about secondary qualities. We decide that something is yellow on the basis of how it looks to us. But sometimes we believe that a thing is not yellow, although it looks yellow; and at other times we believe that a thing is yellow though it does not look yellow. Our beliefs about what things really are yellow would seem to be based on how things look to us under 'standard conditions' of observation; which include both conditions 'external' to the observer, such as the kind of light in which the observation is made, and conditions 'internal' to the observer, such as state of health. It would appear that the subjective theory could make use of an analogue to the colour case to explain our belief that there are 'veridical' and 'non-veridical' judgements of value. Affective responses entirely attributable to, say, preoccupation with one's own worth or loyalty to the value of one's own group might be deemed non-veridical, while those made when no such conditions were operative might be deemed 'veridical'.

The final difficulty concerns the practical implications of the subjective view. Philosophers who take this view are apt to suppose that their scepticism about non-subject-dependent values, as a philosophical position, makes no difference in practical life. Thus Mackie says: 'the lack of objective values is *not* a good reason for abandoning subjective concern or for ceasing to want anything.'[8] And Simon Blackburn says:

It is not initially so surprising that we can go on valuing the good things of life whilst knowing that the valuing is an expression of our own subjective sentiments. This need be no more odd than that we should go on finding things funny or painful, or worthwhile, or beautiful . . . although we accept subjective responses as the source of these reactions.[9]

But it is doubtful whether it does make so little difference.

It is not so uncommon for us to come to view a past, or even a present, belief of ours about the value of something as due to the projection of an affective state of mind. For example, I may think that there is something especially attractive about the familiar neighbourhood of my childhood when I return to it after a long absence. But I may also realise that this response is simply due to the contingency that I happened to have a happy childhood there, and that for anyone lacking such a special connection, i.e. for anyone viewing it 'objectively', the neighbourhood is ordinary and uninteresting. Indeed I may, while realising this, still find the neighbourhood attractive, but if I see the situation like this I shall not claim that the neighbourhood is of any value in itself. So it would seem that when we do understand an attribution of value in the way the subjective theory proposes, as dependent on a contingent-affective response, this is just when we discount it, and do not believe that the thing in question is of intrinsic value.

There is a further aspect of this matter. On the subjective view, a belief that a certain thing has a non-subject-dependent property of intrinsic value is an illusion produced by our affective responses. This, it might be thought, would incline us to take less seriously our beliefs about what is of value. But subjectivists say that we can go on taking them just as seriously as if they were not an illusion. Perhaps a subjectivist again could press an analogy with secondary qualities. Even though philosophical reflection may convince us that 'yellow' is not a property inhering in a thing we believe to be yellow, why should this make any practical difference to us? It does not make us, in practice, see yellow things in a new way. So why should one's belief that something is valuable in itself be seen in some new way just because one accepts the subjective view?

I think there still is a difference. In the case of 'yellow' it does not matter for practical life whether we say that things really are yellow, or instead say that that is how most people take them to be. The latter will do just as well for co-ordinating our activities and for determining the truth or falsity of our beliefs. It could perhaps be, in a similar way, that if our affective responses were sufficiently alike we would have all we needed for co-ordinating the ends we have in practical life, and for establishing criteria for the truth and falsity of beliefs about intrinsic value. But it would seem that we are not only interested in co-ordinating our beliefs about intrinsic value with those of others, but also in whether what we believe to be of intrinsic value really is so. We appear to be concerned that what we suppose to be intrinsically good should be so from a universal point of view.

I have suggested that the subjective view does not fit our experiences of finding things to be of intrinsic value. This, indeed, is conceded: the subjective view is not 'empiricist' in the sense of being based on common experience: it claims that such experiences are systematically mistaken. Experience is rejected because it is inconsistent with a view about what could possibly exist: a view implying that there could not be a property of intrinsic value. If an objective view is to appear plausible, the subjectivist's confidence in his ontological convictions must be eroded.

A belief that something is of intrinsic value is to be understood as the belief that something possesses a certain non-subject-dependent property, i.e. a property analogous to a primary quality. It is not suggested, of course, that it is a regular primary quality, like mass, but that the kind of property it is should be regarded as analogous to a primary quality. The experience we have of something may lead us to postulate that it has such a property in a way analogous to that in which our observations may lead us to postulate that something is, say, spherical. It is true that we do not directly observe that something is of intrinsic value any more than we directly observe that something is spherical. In this respect the subjectivist tradition has been partly correct. Hume said[10] that we do not observe the beauty of a circle, and that is true if it is taken to mean no more than that beauty is not a directly observed property. Hume, of course, thought that the conclusion to be drawn from this was that the beauty of the circle is the projection of an internal sentiment, whereas I would say that the claim that the circle is beautiful is the hypothesis that the circle possesses a certain non-subject-dependent property.

Such an objective approach allows that intrinsic value could be 'part of the fabric of the world', but it is not implied that ethical properties are also. One reason for distinguishing between the practical (including the ethical) and the notion of intrinsic value is that the former is related to the guidance of conduct, while there may be no such connection in the case of the latter. Believing that something is of intrinsic value has no direct implications for how one ought to act. In unfavourable circumstances a person may be mostly concerned with how to survive rather than with what is of intrinsic value. Even in favourable circumstances, when a person's practical ends are more likely to be related to what he believes to be worth while in itself, he may not have the opportunity to give attention to all those things he believes to be of value. While there would seem to be no essential competition to gain a place within the category of what is of intrinsic value, in that the success of one candidate does not have to displace another, there may be competition for a place in our practical projects between those things we believe to be of intrinsic value.

In this connection we may note that something's being intrinsically good does not imply that it is good without qualification. Suppose something A which would be intrinsically good can be brought into existence only at the cost of the destruction of something else B which is intrinsically good. This would not be a reason for doubting the intrinsic goodness of either A or B, but it would be a reason for doubting that both are good without qualification. To say of something that it is good without qualification is a practical judgement: it suggests that it is good from all points of view. It is an overall assessment of how one good thing relates to others, whereas something's being intrinsically good is one possible element within such an overall assessment.

We must now consider how my position is to cope with some obvious objections. On my view assertions that something is of intrinsic value are true or false in virtue of their possession (or otherwise) of a non-subject-dependent property of intrinsic value. The first difficulty concerns how this supposed non-subject-dependent property is meant to be related to regular secondary qualities, such as colour, sound, and texture. Suppose the property of intrinsic value supervenes upon regular secondary qualities. This seems plausible if we reflect that we could not vary the colours, textures, etc. of a painting indefinitely without this affecting our beliefs as to whether it is of value. But the relationship of supervenience cannot be acceptable, in this context, from the objective point of view. For as the properties upon which intrinsic value is said to supervene are secondary qualities, a property of intrinsic value supervening upon these must also be a subject-dependent property.

As I see this objection, it is like arguing that because our observations of a sphere are subject dependent, its having the property of being a sphere must be subject dependent. The relationship between our experiences of something and its being of intrinsic value is not like that between observing that a horse is black and white and believing it to be piebald. Nevertheless my account of the matter does imply that we cannot, for example, vary the colours, shapes, etc. of a painting indefinitely without making a difference to whether we believe it is of value, just as we cannot vary indefinitely the observations we make of a body without this making a difference to whether we believe it is spherical.

But there is more to the matter than this. When we postulate the presence of a certain primary quality on the basis of our experience of various secondary qualities, it would not seem possible that we should agree with another person on all details concerning the secondary qualities present, and yet disagree about the presence of the primary quality, anyway supposing that the agreement extends over a large set of relevant secondary qualities. When we have agreement on many of the relevant secondary qualities this 'fixes' the primary quality. But if we postulate a 'primary quality' of intrinsic value, it would seem that we have to allow that there still can be disagreement in an analogous situation. For surely two people can be in agreement respecting all the regular secondary qualities something has, and yet be in disagreement respecting its intrinsic value? They agree on its colour, shape, texture, etc., but disagree on its value.

The account of the matter given so far leaves out of account an essential element in arriving at a judgement that something is of intrinsic value: having an appropriate affective response. Thus it can be that two people have the same view of all the secondary qualities a thing has and yet disagree as to its intrinsic value: their affective responses can differ. But they could not have the same relevant affective responses and yet differ as to whether something is of intrinsic value. In the case of regular primary qualities there is no necessary connection between our belief in the presence of such a quality and any particular, or indeed any, affective state of mind. But there is a necessary connection between believing that something is of intrinsic value and certain affective states of mind. We warm to, admire, revere, are attracted towards, and take pleasure in that which we believe to be of intrinsic value.

There is more to be said on how we conceive of the relationship between a belief that something is of intrinsic value and affective responses. It is implausible that whenever a person believes in the intrinsic value of O that person has an appropriate affective response when confronted with O; for a person may, for some extraneous reason, fail to have the appropriate affective response on certain occasions. People also believe things to be of intrinsic value on the basis of hearsay: they accept the judgement of a tradition without having formed an independent belief by direct confrontation with O. The correct account may go something like this: if P has an independently warranted belief that something is of intrinsic value, then P must have had, and continue to have, in suitable circumstances, an appropriate affective response when confronted with O.

The second objection, to put it as Mackie would have done,[11] is that intrinsic value would be, on my account, a 'queer' quality, in that it would have no role to play in causal explanations. To consider this difficulty it is necessary to be more explicit about the notion of a primary quality we need for an objective account of intrinsic value. The notion of a primary quality being employed is formally similar to that which would have a role in Bernard Williams's 'absolute conception' of scientific enquiry.[12] Williams advances three main contentions concerning scientific enquiry. (1) Ideally scientific enquiry converges on a single answer to any question about how the physical world is. This answer represents how things 'really are'. (2) Scientific enquiry aims to give us a representation of the world independent of our particular perceptual apparatus as human beings, and the particular place we happen to occupy in the universe. (3) The absolute conception can explain why we have the particular perceptions we do, and why observers constituted differently from us would have the ones they would have.

Questions about the plausibility of Williams's 'absolute conception' as an account of scientific enquiry would be out of place here. My interest lies only in the fact that this account of the absolute conception provides a suitable notion of a primary quality for use in an objective theory of intrinsic value. While the presence of a secondary quality depends upon the particular perceptual apparatus and location of an observer, the presence of a primary quality does not. As every observation we make does depend on our particular perceptual capacities and on our location, the presence of a primary quality cannot be directly observed. It is 'constructed' from our observations.

The primary qualities Williams has in mind in expounding the absolute conception are the regular ones used in scientific explanation. A supposed primary quality of intrinsic value would not be one of those. It would be a quality standing in a similar formal relationship to our observations, in that the intrinsic value of something would not be dependent on our particular perceptual apparatus or on our location in a particular cultural tradition. But it would be of a different substantive character. Now someone of Mackie's point of view would say that while regular primary qualities have a role to play in causal explanations, my supposed primary quality of intrinsic value could not.

This raises the daunting issue of whether, and if so, in what sense, it is necessary that we conceive of the world in terms of the regular primary qualities. If we were to decide that the organization of our experience in terms of those qualities were ultimately grounded on an interest in causally explaining and manipulating physical events, we might note that an alternative conceptual organization would be desirable from the point of view of an interest in what is good in itself. From the point of view of the latter interest an account in terms of the regular primary qualities is quite unilluminating. Certainly a primary quality of intrinsic value would have no part to play in such causal explanations, but then it would not be proposed from the point of view of such an interest.

There is, however, a further problem with this position. Regular primary qualities can be used in explanations of why we experience the secondary qualities we do when placed in certain situations. But how can postulating a 'primary quality' of intrinsic value explain the 'perceptions' we have of intrinsic value? We do not have an account of how a 'primary quality' of intrinsic value *causes* the appropriate affective response. Can such an account be dispensed with? Apparently not, for if those affective responses are not in some sense due to, or caused by, a thing's having the 'primary quality' of intrinsic value, then they are not 'veridical' perceptions of its being of intrinsic value. Suppose you have a certain affective response towards *O* such that you come to believe that *O* is of intrinsic value. Now suppose that although *O* indeed does possess the 'primary quality' of intrinsic value, your affective response is not caused by that, but by something else, say by how *O* impinges on your particular interests. (You do not realise this is why you believe *O* to be of intrinsic value.) This is not then properly a 'perception' of intrinsic value. So it would seem that we do need to claim that a 'veridical' perception of intrinsic value is one that is due to the intrinsic value *O* has. But this 'due to' cannot be a regular causal story, making use of regular primary qualities. Then what kind of causal relationship is involved? Is it a different kind of causal relationship from that involved in scientific explanation? I cannot see how to take this matter further.

The final difficulty to be considered concerns the relationship between the proposed property of intrinsic value and experience. What experiences must we have to make it reasonable to believe that something is of intrinsic value? It is plausible, as the subjectivist tradition has maintained, that the presence of certain colours, shapes, sounds, and textures may be agreed without this implying agreement on the presence of value. It would also seem that the occurrence of some affective response is internally related to having the belief that something is of intrinsic value. On the subjective view it is assumed that if responses are affective they cannot also provide us with evidence of the character of that which produces the response (other than its propensity to produce such a response). But it is unclear why affective responses cannot be cognitive in character.

It may be said that affective responses are subject dependent: their occurrence and character depend on what we are like and the circumstances in which we are placed, as well as on the object of the response. But this is also true of the experiences upon which we base claims about the presence of the regular primary qualities. It is true that often we have difficulty in telling whether affective responses are distorted by our practical situation and interests. But in some cases, at least, it seems unlikely that they are, for much the same response may be produced despite considerable changes in personal situation and concerns. The crucial evidence from which we construct the hypothesis that something is of intrinsic value is a certain type of affective response.

Thus it is possible to incorporate within an objective view a point traditionally stressed by subjectivists: that certain affective responses are necessarily related to the belief that something is of intrinsic value. But these affective responses take the role of evidence for the presence of value, not of themselves being what is of intrinsic value (as classical utilitarians would claim regarding pleasure), or of producing the illusion that their objects are of value. Affective responses are the evidence on which we base first-hand opinions about what is of intrinsic value. The occurrence of desire sometimes can be taken as the discovery of the value of the object of desire. Thus, if people are to have well-founded views about what is of intrinsic value, it is necessary that they should have the right to experiment with different 'modes of existence'. If a state or a society takes a constricted view of desirable 'modes of existence', making it difficult for anyone to live in other than one of a few acceptable ways, members of that society will be prevented from experiencing new 'modes of existence', some of which may have contained something of worth.

It is said that if something is of intrinsic value then it is of value in itself. A person's desiring O could not make O of intrinsic value. Now it may be thought that this raises a difficulty for my defence of liberalism. Many of the things people desire as worth having for their own sakes are things each person desires for himself, such as wealth and success. A person does not usually desire that people generally should be wealthy or successful, but that *he* should be these things. Then must we say that people who have such desires are necessarily mistaken about what is of intrinsic value? If we do say this, then what is to become of the doctrine that people ought to enjoy rights of self-ownership so that they can have more reasonable views about what is worth while in itself? It would seem that the 'discoveries' of many people can be discounted in advance, because we know, from what is implied by the concept of intrinsic value, that they must be mistaken. Why should people be at liberty to pursue such necessarily mistaken conceptions of what is worth while in itself?

This is a misinterpretation of the beliefs of those who think that wealth and success are of intrinsic value. It is true that if P thinks that O is of intrinsic value, then P cannot think O's being of value depends on whether P desires O. That is to say, P cannot think that his simply desiring O is what makes O of intrinsic value. Of course P may be an egomaniac who supposes that *he* would not be mistaken in thinking something was of intrinsic value (i.e. *his* desires are always for the right things), but that is not the same as thinking that one's desire for O confers intrinsic value on O. But one can desire O for oneself (and not for others) without thinking that O's being of value is dependent on one's desiring it. And this would be the correct way of describing many people's desire for wealth and success: P desires success for P, but P does not think that the desirability of success is dependent on P desiring it. If Q has success and P does not, P thinks what Q has is a desirable thing, though P desires P's having this desirable thing, not Q's having it. It is true that P cannot think that P's having success is of intrinsic value, but P does not have to suppose that.

Therefore I can consistently allow that people should have the right to choose such things as wealth and success as being of intrinsic value. As a matter of fact I think that those who regard wealth and success as of intrinsic value are mistaken. But their being mistaken is not simply an implication of what it means to say that something is of intrinsic value: it is something that is discovered by people experimenting with 'modes of existence' in which these things figure prominently, and ones in which they do not.

It might be thought that if attention is to be given to the discernment, creation, and preservation of what is intrinsically good, it would also be appropriate to be concerned about the reduction or elimination of what is intrinsically bad. This thought could be provoked by the reflection that it would be curious for a hedonist to be concerned about the promotion of pleasure, while indifferent to the occurrence of pain, even though it is true that the mere absence of pain is not a species of pleasure. It is unclear what can be meant by saying that something is intrinsically bad other than that, judged from the point of view of its intrinsic worth, it is very much lacking. Such judgements would usually be made of those things created with the intention that they should be intrinsically good, and which have conspicuously failed to be so. The question whether there is anything intrinsically bad should be separated from the question whether evil exists. Evil is a moral notion; indicating the will to being something about, or to delight in something, because of its moral perversity. Now as moral good and bad are relational notions, depending on our characteristics as human beings, that which is evil is not, because of its being evil, intrinsically bad.

It would seem possible that there should be degrees of intrinsic value. One thing may be of intrinsic value, but of less intrinsic value than another. There is no obvious reason why everything which is of intrinsic value must be very grand. Why should it not be that some quite small and transient thing is of intrinsic value?

Lack of knowledge of what is of intrinsic value

I have tried to sketch and defend an objectivist view of intrinsic value, suitable for use in my defence of liberalism. The attempt to gain more reasonable views about what is valuable or worth while in itself is not futile, as a subjectivist theory would imply. It must also be shown, however, that such an attempt is not redundant. For some, while agreeing that claims about intrinsic value are objective, would go further and say that we already know what is of intrinsic value. I shall now try to show that these claims cannot be sustained.

It is not said that we lack knowledge of all forms of goodness. It has already been allowed that we can have knowledge of what is instrumentally good, though such knowledge is subject dependent. There are also plausible proposals about what is good for human beings. One form such proposals might take is of an intuitively plausible list; for example, life, continued physical and mental health, freedom from incapacitation, pain, pressing material need, and confinement, the society of others, and security in the enjoyment of these goods. It may be allowed that from the point of view of a normal person in normal circumstances these are good things to have. It may be, too, that sufficient agreement could be reached on a set of proposals along these lines to serve as the basis for a maximand in a consequentialist ethic. Though there will be two problems with this. One of the goods on this list may in practice come into conflict with one or more of the rest, in the sense that what is to be done to secure the better provision of one will cause a worse provision of another. Secondly, the provision of one of these goods to some may make it less likely that they can be provided to others. An alternative and more methodical approach to establishing a set of goods is to propose a principle for generating a suitable list, such as Rawls's 'primary goods': those things it is rational to want whatever else one wants.[13]

The point about both of these approaches – the un-systematic and the systematic – is that they do not contain plausible suggestions about what is of intrinsic value (Rawls does not suggest, of course, that the primary goods are such a suggestion: a person's views as to what is of intrinsic value are presumably a part of his 'full' conception of his own good.) They are not plausible proposals about what is of intrinsic value for this reason. If something is of intrinsic value, then its goodness is non-relational. But the goodness of things on these lists is relational. Though any normal person in normal circumstances will consider it good to continue to live, say, it is nevertheless a relational judge-ment, in that if continuing to live were to come to involve too much physical or mental suffering it would be intelligible for a person to regard it as no longer having value. Rawls's primary goods are also relational goods. Let us set aside the common criticism that there are 'full' conceptions of a person's good such that it would not be rational to want some of the primary goods. Let us suppose, with Rawls, that it is rational to want his list of primary goods whatever else one wants. What this means is that the goodness of the primary goods is not conditional upon the specific content of any person's full conception of his own good. It does not mean that the primary goods are unconditional in another sense, viz. that one has reason to want them whatever one's circumstances of life. For a person might have no 'full' conception of his own good he wished to pursue – he might be bored or disgusted with life, and therefore lack reason to regard the primary goods as goods. In this sense the goodness of the primary goods is relational, and the primary goods could not, therefore, be of intrinsic value. (Which is not to deny, of course, that normally the appropriate relations hold, and that they are good.)

My intention has not been to quibble over whether the goods we have been discussing are 'objective': only to show that they are not plausibly intrinsic goods. Let us turn, then, to some traditional claims to know what is of intrinsic value. The most famous, that of classical utilitarianism, has been to say that those things that are of intrinsic value (and the only things that are of intrinsic value) are certain states of mind of sentient beings, such as pleasure. This position appears to have advantages over both the 'objective' and the 'subjective' views of intrinsic value. Like subjectivism, it accepts that if there were no sentient beings there would be nothing of intrinsic value, though for a different reason. It would not be because there would be no affective states to produce the illusion of things having intrinsic value, but because none of those states of mind of intrinsic value would exist. The 'state of mind' view can also account for the conviction that for something to have intrinsic value it must affect us in some way; though strictly it will not be those things that affect us that are of intrinsic value, but the states of mind produced in us. And it avoids the scepticism of the subjective view: that really nothing is of intrinsic value – that it is only an illusion produced by our affective responses. For on the 'state of mind' view we are supposed to know that certain states of mind have intrinsic value. Thus E. J. Bond says of pleasure that it is 'inherently good, or good in virtue of its very nature; it is furthermore a kind of value that can be immediately felt, acknowledged, recognized.'[14]

Obviously not every state of mind is a plausible candidate for that which we know to have intrinsic value. It could not be any of those states of mind we find disagreeable, such as anxiety, but only one or more of those states we look upon favourably, such as pleasure, or feeling happy. It would appear that it must also be an 'affective' state of mind, rather than one of those states, such as 'thinking about *p*', which leaves it an open matter what, if any, affective response we might have. It may be noted that a proposal along these lines as to what we know to be of intrinsic value does not have to be limited to one affective state of mind. It is not clear why the claims of nostalgia or elation should be any less good as candidates for what has intrinsic value than the claims of pleasure. Classical utilitarianism attempted a reduction to only one state of mind because it wanted to propose a decision procedure for ethics, and there would be obvious problems for this ambition if it were said that more than one kind of thing is intrinsically valuable. But it should be noted that such an attempt at reduction is not implied by the suggestion that states of mind are of intrinsic value: that thesis is quite compatible with pluralism about what is of intrinsic value.

I shall consider the claim that we know that pleasure is intrinsically good. The arguments against this claim can be extended to cover any other state of mind which might be proposed as intrinsically good. The argument against pleasure being intrinsically good is based on the point that if something is intrinsically good, then its goodness is non-relational. The goodness of pleasure, however, is relational: for example, it depends on the value we place on the source of the pleasure. One may experience pleasure from satisfying a desire for an addictive drug. It is quite intelligible that someone should experience pleasure when the craving is satisfied, and also believe that that experience is of no value in itself. If the addiction were cured, the addict could quite intelligibly take the view that the cure was not at the expense of anything valuable: that nothing of value had been taken from his life. A similar observation can be made about taking pleasure in degrading others. If a person has taken pleasure in doing this, and then repents, it would not be appropriate for that person to see the situation as one where he now does the morally appropriate thing at the cost of giving up something valuable. If he repents, he will no longer see that pleasure as of value in itself.

The point here is not that the experiencing of certain pleasures may in fact adversely affect other things one finds value in, such as one's health. That would not be an argument against pleasure being of intrinsic value, because it is not entailed by something's being intrinsically good that it is good without qualification. The point of these examples is that they are cases where we may think pleasure is of no value at all, which shows that the value of pleasure is relational: it depends on the value we place on the source of the pleasure. Nor is it my point that we do not always have reason to pursue an opportunity for pleasure. There is nothing in this incompatible with the view that pleasure is desirable in itself; for, in general, we do not always have reason to pursue that which is desirable in itself, when the cost in terms of other things is taken into account. My point is that pleasurable experiences are not of intrinsic value.

This argument needs to be supplemented with an explanation of why it should have been so commonly thought that pleasure is of intrinsic value. Consider someone who said 'I have pleasurable experiences from time to time, but unlike you, I want them to stop as soon as possible.' This, he explains, is not because he is a puritan, who has pleasurable experiences and finds them agreeable, but thinks it wicked to have them. It is because he finds having pleasurable experiences disagreeable. We would conclude that whatever the state of mind this person is referring to, it is not the type we refer to as 'pleasurable experience'. For we cannot have a pleasurable experience without finding it attractive and wishing it to continue. It would seem that the attractiveness of pleasure, which is a necessary characteristic of pleasure, is confused with its being intrinsically desirable. It does not follow from pleasure necessarily being attractive that it is desirable in itself; for that which is not desirable in itself, and which we recognise to be not desirable in itself (for example, taking a drug) may attract us.

The 'state of mind' view does not give us knowledge of what is of intrinsic value. It may also be noticed that it does not fulfil its initial promise of avoiding what some would say is a problem with an 'objectivist' view of intrinsic value: that it requires us to attribute a 'queer' property to things of intrinsic value. For the 'state of mind' view does have to attribute such a property to states of mind. The view is not that intrinsic value is (say) pleasure (which would be absurd), but that pleasure has the property of being intrinsically valuable. So if there are any problems about the attribution of a property of intrinsic value, they are problems for the 'state of mind' view too. The value pleasure has is, according to this 'state of mind' position, not subject dependent. Of course there must be subjects in which pleasurable states occur. And what 'external' things give rise to pleasurable experience may vary from person to person. But the truth of the claim that pleasure is intrinsically valuable is not intended to be subject dependent: it does not depend on what attitude a person takes towards his pleasures. On the classical utilitarian view the pleasures of a puritan are intrinsically valuable, despite the unfavourable attitude the puritan may take towards them.

The underlying argument against the proposal that we know pleasure (or, for that matter, any other state of mind) to be of intrinsic value is that the value of pleasure is relational. The same underlying argument will dispose of the claim that happiness is of intrinsic value. We are not thinking here of happiness as a transient state of mind or mood: that would be merely a further form of the 'state of mind' view. Let us, rather, take happiness in a 'long-term' sense, where we may say that for a person to be happy he must believe that his circumstances are satisfactory or good by reference to his principal ends.[15] The value of a person's happiness will depend on what is the nature of those ends. If we think that they are trivial or crazy, or if we think that they are wicked, we shall not think of the happiness of the person having those ends as of value, even if he correctly believes that his life goes well by reference to those ends. Suppose a man who is mentally ill is happy because he is able to pursue some crazy ends to his satisfaction. He then recovers and sees that those ends were crazy. He (and we) do not think that something of value is lost, in that the old happiness is now gone. The same might be said of the now remorseful war criminal who had been happy pursuing the degradation of his victims.

My position on the intrinsic value of states of mind and happiness invites a query. Surely everyone thinks that various pleasures (according to his taste) and being happy are good things. And these things are not generally thought to be a means to something else desirable: they are regarded as desirable in themselves. Must it not be, then, that these things are of intrinsic value?

It is not denied that certain states of mind and happiness are desirable in a non-instrumental way. My claim is that it does not follow from that that they are intrinsically desirable. In the case of pleasure we find it desirable because, necessarily, we are attracted to what we believe will bring us pleasure. Happiness, too, in so far as it is a state of mind, necessarily attracts us; and furthermore, it must be that we derive satisfaction from the successful pursuit of those goals we consider to be worth while. Here we have the explanations of why we find pleasure and happiness good in a non-instrumental way.

But to this it might be replied 'So much the worse, then, for the idea of intrinsic value.' Is there any need to suppose that there are things of intrinsic value? There does seem to be a distinction between what people want wholly as a means to something else, and what they want, wholly or partly, for itself. An existence in which everything desired is desired as a means to something else is generally regarded as very unsatisfactory. (For example, imagine yourself in a situation where everything you do you do as a means to staying alive.) Now consider those things people want wholly or partly for themselves. Do they have to regard these things as of intrinsic value in the way I have suggested; i.e. as things the value of which is non-relational? Suppose it is allowed that the value these things have for them is due to certain likings and desires they happen to have (and that these are due to fortuitous circumstances, such as the nature of human desires, or their individual desires, or the location they happen to have in a cultural tradition, or what happens to be the fashionable view.) Should that make these things any less attractive? If I like chocolate and the cat doesn't, why should the thought that if I were the cat I wouldn't like chocolate make me get any less pleasure out of eating chocolate? It is sad if a person finds nothing desirable in itself. But must that be how a person finds things if he/she believes that the value anything has for him/her is relational?

There are two kinds of extrinsic value. (1) The value of O is extrinsic because it has its value (for some given person(s)) only because it can contribute to the bringing about of P, which they want. (2) The value of O is extrinsic because it would not have the value it has for some given person(s) if they did not desire it in a certain way. It would be unsatisfactory to say that all value is extrinsic (1), but not obvious why it should be unsatisfactory to say that all value is extrinsic in either sense (1) or sense (2). So it could be that no value is intrinsic.

The mere fact that we find that something O attracts us does not strike us as sufficient reason to be concerned with it. It may be suggested that the reason for this is that before we have reason to be concerned with it we have to fit it into a scheme including all the things that attract us. Concern with O may be eliminated because of the sacrifices of other things that attract us which would be necessary in order to pursue O. But sometimes we eliminate O without thought of these further implications. For example, even if we are fascinated by watching drops form and fall from a tap, we are unlikely to make this activity a major part of our lives. Is this because the attractiveness of O is not confirmed by current views of what is of worth? No doubt this is often the reason. But then we can raise questions about the soundness of these current views, and thus we return to the concept of intrinsic value. (From the point of view of most of us, we shall simply see ourselves as confronted with competing current views of what is of worth, and as having to make choices between them.)

It has been argued that pleasure and happiness could not be of intrinsic value because their value is relational: dependent on the source of the pleasure or happiness. This argument is a priori: it rests on what it is to say that something is of intrinsic value, and does not depend on experience of pleasure or happiness; on, for example, becoming disillusioned with the pursuit of pleasure. Now many people, apparently, pursue pleasure and happiness in the (for me mistaken) belief that they are of worth in themselves. Why should this pursuit be allowed (as it is by the universal assignment of rights of self-ownership) if it can be known in advance that it must be futile?

It would be absurdly puritanical to be concerned about the harmless pursuit of pleasure, even if the source of the pleasure could not be regarded as of intrinsic value. But pleasure, and similar affective responses, are indispensable for the appreciation of what is worth while in itself. To forbid the pursuit of pleasure (if that were possible) would not only prevent people from following a mistaken view of what is of intrinsic value, but also prevent them from ever arriving at any well-founded views of what is worth while in itself.

Turning to the case of happiness, it is to be expected that everyone in normal circumstances will pursue his/her own happiness, as a person will wish to be in circumstances of life which are good or satisfactory from the point of view of his/her principal ends. (It is not said that *necessarily* a person pursues his/her own happiness, because in some cases a single highly valued goal may be pursued at the expense of others a person has, in such a way as to make happiness unlikely.) There is a contrast between the pursuit of pleasure and the pursuit of happiness. It is possible to take pleasure in something one thinks to be of no value (apart from its giving one pleasure of a certain kind). In the case of happiness, however, one must regard those goals or standards by reference to which one judges one's circumstances of life as desirable or worth while in some way. While a person does not have to believe that these ends are of intrinsic value, people often think they are. It would be impossible to discourage the pursuit of happiness without also discouraging the pursuit of certain goals which those who have them believe to be of value in themselves, i.e. without discouraging the pursuit of what is worth while in itself.

It is not possible to anticipate and consider every proposal that might be made as to what we know to be of intrinsic value. It seems likely, however, that further proposals will also fail because they too turn out to be relational goods. For example, it might be suggested that rational practical activity, or the capacity to undertake such activity, is of intrinsic value. But evidently, if such activity is directed to a wicked or a worthless end we do not consider it, or the capacity to engage in it, to be of the same value as if it were directed at a good or worth while end. Or it might be suggested that the satisfaction of preferences is intrinsically good. But this suggestion gains any plausibility it might have either because of the thought that preference satisfaction is desirable for hedonistic reasons (you have the pleasure of satisfying your desire), or because a person's preferences are thought of as expressing the determinations of practical rationality. Both suggestions have already been disposed of.

So far we have considered claims to know what is of intrinsic value where it is assumed that what is of intrinsic value will be anything falling within a certain category – for example, pleasurable experience. There is an altogether different approach to claims to know what is of intrinsic value: to claim that we know that particular things, for example, *War and Peace*, are of intrinsic value. We might give up attempts to find a formula for what is of intrinsic value, and instead simply list those particular things which are of intrinsic value.

Are there particular things concerning which we can say 'We know that this is of intrinsic value'? Any claim that some particular thing is of intrinsic value is open to the following source of doubt. In the past we have been confident that some particular thing was intrinsically good. Later we have had to revise that belief. We have come to see

that the belief that it was of intrinsic value is wholly
explicable by reference to some extraneous desire, such as
the wish to be thought fashionable in one's opinions. Now
consider the things you currently think to be intrinsically
good. These beliefs too may later prove to have been wholly
explicable in terms of extraneous desires. Thus we cannot
claim to know that any particular thing is of intrinsic value.

What, though, if there is a widespread consensus within a
certain culture that something is of intrinsic value? Would
not this make it very probable that the thing is of intrinsic
value? It is possible that there should be collective as well as
individual mistakes about what is of intrinsic value. Collective mistakes can become apparent to later generations.
Consider the emphasis placed on elaborate dress, entertain-
ment, and manners by the European upper-middle-class
culture of the late nineteenth century. At that time it was
thought worth while to do these things for their own sake: to
later generations it has seemed ridiculous – to be explained,
perhaps, by the extraneous desire to display wealth.

Nevertheless within a particular cultural tradition there
does emerge, over time, a consensus that certain things are
of intrinsic value: and the longer this consensus lasts, the
better reason we have for trusting these judgements, even if
we never actually achieve certainty. Certain works in drama
and philosophy, for example, have now endured for more
than two millennia, and have been admired from a great
variety of cultural locations and current practical preoccupa-
tions. It is by now very unlikely that these favourable
judgements are due to the existence of extraneous desires.

So let it be allowed that some of our beliefs about what is
of intrinsic value are very probably true. It is not plausible
that what any one of us believes to be of intrinsic value, or
what is recognized now as having intrinsic value within a
certain tradition, represents all those things which are of
intrinsic value. A given cultural tradition creates new
things, some of which come to be recognised as of value.
Thus we cannot know now all those things which will be
thought to be of value. This is not a matter merely of new

examples being created within an established cultural tradition, but also of the creation of new traditions, for example, of opera at the end of the sixteenth century, containing new possibilities of works of value.

We may conclude, therefore, that it is not the case that we already know (everything) that is of intrinsic value. Therefore the assignment of a liberal set of individual rights in order to make possible more reasonable views about what is worth while in itself is not redundant.

Postscript

If it is maintained that one reason for upholding rights of self-ownership, and hence the liberal rights and freedoms, is that respect for those rights makes it likely that we shall have more reasonable views about what is worth while in itself, it might be expected that some evidence will be produced that this is so. In chapter 3 I evaded this issue by saying that any attempt to produce evidence of such a connection must rest on assuming contestable views about what is worth while in itself. Obviously if you and I have different views about what activities are worth while in themselves, then although we may agree on which activities have flourished and which declined, we may disagree on whether this represents progress towards the discovery of what is worth while in itself. In chapter 3 there followed an attempt to justify a connection between upholding rights of self-ownership and the discovery of what is worth while in itself which avoided the acceptance of a particular set of views about what is worth while in itself. However, the credibility of my position for any particular reader will be influenced by his or her view of what is worth while in itself, and whether those things have flourished under the liberal rights and liberties.

My position does not imply that there will be continuing progress towards better conceptions of what is worth while in itself. This form of liberalism is not in the business of historical prediction: it does not say that there will be progress in the direction of more respect for rights of self-ownership. (It is difficult to understand how anyone could embark on historical prediction at the present time, when the future of most of mankind could be affected so drastically and unpredictably by the decisions of so few people.) The theory gives one reason why there ought to be rights of self-ownership. It says that if the liberal rights and liberties are generally respected we shall come to have more reasonable views about what is worth while. If it were thought, on the contrary, that the exercise of choice under the liberal freedoms has led to ever more trivial modes of existence, my conception of liberalism would not be very plausible. Sympathy might turn towards some form of authoritarian conservatism: those still retaining a sense of what is worth while should seek to preserve what is good in the past from the encroachments of trivial popular taste.

The question turns, then, on (1) whether respect for the liberal rights and liberties prevails, and (2) if so, whether progress towards more reasonable views of what is worth while is discernible. It is scarcely contestable that in the West in the last few decades the idea that legal and social relations ought to be governed by respect for rights of self-ownership has become more influential. The idea that a person's 'plan for life' should be the outcome of his or her exercises of rights of self-ownership, rather than conformity to obligations which already exist independent of the agent's will, has clearly gained ground. For example, people once often thought themselves to be tied to a particular location and nation by sentiment and loyalty. Now they are apt to regard themselves as free to choose where they will live on the basis of employment prospects, congenial society, cultural interests, climate, and so on; with choice at any particular time always open to revision. Again there has been an erosion in the sense of obligation to others, where that obligation is not grounded in voluntary agreement: for example, the obligation of children to care for their parents if in need of care, or the obligation of children to respect their parents' aspirations for them in careers or marriage.

Even in some cases where obligations are based on agreement, as in marriage, there is a tendency to reject the claims of a voluntary undertaking if it proves onerous.

It may now be said that although the rights of self-ownership the liberal recommends have gained increasing recognition in the West, there is no reason to suppose that this has been accompanied by more secure discernment of what is worth while in itself. On the contrary, the rise in respect for rights of self-ownership seems to many to have been accompanied by a decline in the civilisation of the West. Our concert halls and opera houses normally perform works written in the last century or earlier, impressionism is the most recent popular style in painting, and our most admired architecture was built 150 years or more ago. We have none of that sense of doing better than ever before to be found amongst the painters and sculptors of fifteenth-century Florence or the musicians of late-eighteenth-century Vienna. The common judgement is that, except technically, our culture is past the peak of its achievements.

It would be easier to defend my form of liberalism against this pessimistic view if I were inclined to question it in one of the usual ways – for example, 'we are not yet in a position to assess what are the good things of our own time.' But I am not. So it is time to make excuses. For a start, we must distinguish between having more reasonable views about what is worth while, and our ability to match our creations to this discernment. While our ability to create what is worth while may have declined, it is not implausible that the ability to discern what is worth while has increased. And two further reasons might be mentioned why the increased acknowledgement of rights of self-ownership in the West has not been accompanied by an impressive period of Western civilisation.

Although people have had greater time and energy to devote to activities they consider to be worth while for their own sake, and have made choices in a freer environment, generally they have had little education in the traditions of their culture. This is probably part of the explanation of why low-level leisure activities, such as TV soap operas and spectator sports, are currently so popular. By contrast, the aristocracy and the upper bourgeoisie of two centuries ago took a cultural education for granted. The other reason has been the preoccupation, for two centuries, with improvements in the instrumental aspects of life. As substantial gains have been possible here, and further ones have continued to seem likely, inventive talent has been attracted in this direction. By contrast, up until two centuries ago, instrumental advances had been infrequent, and the prospects for additional ones seemed poor. It was reasonable to suppose that the instrumental aspects of human life could not be improved upon significantly, and had to be taken as they were. Inventiveness was apt to be applied to what was believed to be worth while in itself.

At some time in the future the situation may return to how it has been throughout most of human history: little prospect of anything more than slight improvements in the instrumental aspects of human life. Instead of continual revision of the instrumental aspects of our lives, there again may be stability in this sphere. This could be because the best instrumental solution already had been found (e.g. the eradication of smallpox), or because so close an approximation to the optimal solution had been found that further progress was uninteresting. Or it could be just that no answers seemed to be in sight to the theoretical problems blocking further advance in instrumental techniques. If such a stage were reached it might be expected that more innovative talent would be applied to activities considered to be worth while for their own sake.

These are my excuses. One cannot make excuses for ever. If rights of self-ownership continue to be respected, there should come a point at which there is general confidence that progress has been made in recognizing what is worth while in itself. If that does not happen, the argument of this book is mistaken.

Notes

Chapter 1 What Liberalism Is

1 John Rawls, *A Theory of Justice*, Oxford, Oxford University Press, 1972, p. 31.
2 J. S. Mill, *On Liberty*, in *Utilitarianism, Liberty and Representative Government*, London, Dent, 1960, p. 75.
3 Rawls, *A Theory of Justice*, p. 61.
4 This has been argued in my 'Rights, Consequences, and Mill on Liberty', in A. Phillips Griffiths (ed.), *Of Liberty*, Cambridge, Cambridge University Press, 1983, pp. 168ff.
5 Immanuel Kant, *The Moral Law* (trans. H. J. Paton), London, Hutchinson, 1956 (3rd edn), p. 96 (Prussian Academy pp. 428–9).
6 Rawls, *A Theory of Justice*, pp. 11ff.
7 See G. A. Cohen, 'Self-Ownership, World-Ownership, and Equality', in F. Lucash (ed.), *Justice and Equality Here and Now*, Ithaca, Cornell University Press, 1986, pp. 109–10.
8 Compare with Cohen, 'Self-Ownership, World-Ownership, and Equality', p. 112.
9 A view endorsed by Hillel Steiner, in 'Liberty and Equality', *Political Studies*, XXIX (1981), 566.
10 This argument is taken from my contribution to the symposium 'Liberty, Equality, Property', in *Proceedings of the Aristotelian Society*, suppl. vol. LV (1981), 179ff.
11 Gerald C. MacCallum, 'Negative and Positive Freedom', in Richard E. Flathman (ed.), *Concepts in Social and Political Philosophy*, New York, Macmillan, 1973, p. 296.
12 An account of liberalism along these lines is adopted by

Cohen, 'Self-Ownership, World-Ownership, and Equality', pp. 108–18.

13 Mill, *On Liberty*, p. 132; Rawls, *A Theory of Justice*, sections 11, 26, and 39.

Chapter 2 Rights and Maximizing Consequentialism

1 Earlier attempts of mine to argue against basing liberalism on conventional forms of consequentialism are: (1) 'Liberalism and Utilitarianism', *Ethics*, 90. 3 (1980), 319–34; and (2) 'Rights, Consequences, and Mill on Liberty', pp. 172–4. These earlier arguments oppose specific forms of consequentialist justification, whereas the present one is intended to be quite general.
2 I owe this suggestion to Stephen Darwall.
3 I owe this suggestion to G. A. Cohen.
4 Gilbert Harman, *The Nature of Morality*, New York, Oxford University Press, 1977, pp. 3–4.
5 T. M. Scanlon, 'Contractualism and Utilitarianism' in Amartya Sen and Bernard Williams (eds), *Utilitarianism and Beyond*, Cambridge, Cambridge University Press, 1982, p. 110.
6 See Bernard Williams, in J. J. C. Smart and Bernard Williams, *Utilitarianism: For and Against*, Cambridge, Cambridge University Press, 1973, pp. 108ff.

Chapter 3 Experimental Consequentialism

1 I owe this point to G. A. Cohen.
2 Robert Nozick, *Anarchy, State and Utopia*, New York, Basic Books, 1974, ch. 7, section I.
3 Mill, *On Liberty*, pp. 129–30.
4 A similar preference, though for different reasons, is expressed in Hillel Steiner, 'Slavery, Socialism and Private Property' in J. R. Pennock and J. W. Chapman (eds), *Nomos XXII*, *Private Property*, New York, New York University Press, 1980.
5 For a different way of putting this problem see my 'Rights, Consequences, and Mill on Liberty', pp. 178ff.

6 I owe this suggestion to G. A. Cohen.
7 Compare with Hillel Steiner, 'The Natural Right to the Means of Production', *Philosophical Quarterly* 27 (1977), 48n.
8 I owe this suggestion to G. A. Cohen.
9 The following example comes from my contribution to the symposium 'Liberty, Equality, Property', pp. 181–3.
10 Compare with Nozick, *Anarchy, State and Utopia*, p. 235.
11 John Gray, *Hayek on Liberty* (2nd edn), Oxford, Blackwell, 1986, p. 101.
12 This problem was drawn to my attention by G. A. Cohen.

Chapter 4 Property

1 A point made by G. A. Cohen, 'Self-Ownership, World-Ownership and Equality: Part II' in *Social Philosophy and Policy*, spring 1986, p. 83.
2 Cohen, 'Self-Ownership, Part II', p. 86, says '. . . what sort of self-ownership do we feel moved to insist that people should enjoy? Is it (1) merely formal self-ownership, that bare bourgeois freedom which distinguishes the most abject proletarian from a slave, or is it (2) a more substantive self-ownership which we can associate with the idea of controlling one's life?'
3 Following on from the discussion in ch. 1 it is assumed that rights of control over material things are natural rights, but 'assigned' not 'perceived' natural rights. In that chapter an argument was offered for why, in general, there could be no perceived natural rights. It was denied that either private-property rights or self-ownership rights were perceived natural rights. Therefore the discussion in this chapter will take the form of considering the reasons for assigning individual private-property rights, and also the reasons against doing so, from the point of view of my overall consequentialist approach. But if it were true that there are perceived natural rights to property, the discussion about how property rights are to be assigned would be inappropriate, for people might already have perceived rights in particular pieces of property, and we would not be free to consider how such rights should be assigned. I do not believe that there are perceived natural rights to property, but shall not argue the point here.

An account of the 'full', or 'liberal' concept of ownership (following A. M. Honoré) is to be found in Lawrence C. Becker, *Property Rights*, London, Routledge and Kegan Paul, 1977, pp. 18ff.

4 What Nozick has taught us is that it will be in keeping with everyone's rights if *that* (implausibly) is what everyone's rights are. See my contribution to the symposium 'Liberty, Equality, Property', pp. 177–8.

5 pp. 160ff.

6 See G. A. Cohen, 'Capitalism, Freedom, and the Proletariat', in Alan Ryan (ed.), *The Idea of Freedom*, Oxford, Oxford University Press, 1979, pp. 10–15; and C. C. Ryan 'Yours, Mine and Ours: Property Rights and Individual Liberty', *Ethics*, 87 (1977), 137–38.

7 'No habitat for a shmoo', *Listener*, 4 Sept. 1986, p. 6; *Karl Marx's Theory of History: A Defence*, Oxford, Clarendon Press, 1978, ch. XI.

8 I owe this point to an observation by Adrian Ryan.

9 See my 'Competitive Equality of Opportunity', *Mind*, LXXXVI (1977), 388.

10 This has been shown by Jennifer Mayor, in her unpublished doctoral dissertation for the CNAA, 1984, 'Property and Welfare in Liberal Political Philosophy'.

Chapter 5 Intrinsic Value

1 See Bernard Williams, 'Ethics and the Fabric of the World', in Ted Honderich (ed.), *Morality and Objectivity*, London, Routledge and Kegan Paul, 1985, p. 206.

2 See E. J. Bond, *Reason and Value*, Cambridge, Cambridge University Press, 1983, p. 96; and Bernard Williams, *Ethics and the Limits of Philosophy*, London, Fontana, 1985, p. 135.

3 J. L. Mackie, *Ethics: Inventing Right and Wrong*, Harmondsworth, Penguin, 1977, pp. 42ff.

4 Robert Nozick, *Philosophical Explanations*, Oxford, Clarendon Press, 1981, p. 422.

5 G. E. Moore, 'The Conception of Intrinsic Value' in *Philosophical Studies*, London, Routledge and Kegan Paul, 1951, p. 260.

6 This and later examples might give the impression that I believe that all cases where things are of intrinsic value are also

cases where they are of aesthetic value. It is not my intention to assert or defend this thesis.

7 Mackie, *Ethics: Inventing Right and Wrong*, p. 35.

8 Mackie, *Ethics: Inventing Right and Wrong*, p. 34.

9 Simon Blackburn, 'Error and the Phenomenology of Value', in Honderich (ed.), *Morality and Objectivity*, p. 10.

10 David Hume, *Enquiry Concerning the Principles of Morals*, appendix I.

11 Mackie, *Ethics: Inventing Right and Wrong*, pp. 38ff.

12 Williams, *Ethics and the Limits of Philosophy*, ch. 8.

13 Rawls, *A Theory of Justice*, p. 62 and section 15. The primary social goods are rights and liberties, powers and opportunities, and income and wealth; and the primary natural goods are health and vigour, and intelligence and imagination.

14 Bond, *Reason and Value*, p. 98.

15 See my 'Happiness', *Philosophical Quarterly*, 18 (1968), 97.

Index

Index by Keith Seddon